THE CATHOLIC HYMN BOOK

A Collection of Hymns, Anthems, Etc.

Published by Left of Brain Books

Copyright © 2021 Left of Brain Books

ISBN 978-1-396-31898-6

First Edition

All rights reserved. No part of this publication may be reproduced, distributed, or transmitted in any form or by any means, including photocopying, recording, or other electronic or mechanical methods, without the prior written permission of the publisher, except in the case of brief quotations embodied in critical reviews and certain other noncommercial uses permitted by copyright law. Left of Brain Books is a division of Left of Brain Onboarding Pty Ltd.

Table of Contents

HYMNS FOR WEEK-DAYS AND SUNDAYS, WHEN NOT OTHERWISE APPOINTED.   1

   Morning Hymns.   1
   Sunday Morning.   3
   Evening Hymns.   5
   Antiphons of the Blessed Virgin. from the First Sunday in Advent to the Feast of the Purification.   8
   From the Purification of the Blessed Virgin to Palm Sunday.   8
   From Easter Sunday to Whitsunday.   9
   From Trinity Sunday to the Last Sunday after Pentecost.   9
   Sundays and Week-Days in Advent.   10

HYMNS FOR THE PRINCIPAL HOLY DAYS AND SAINTS' DAYS.   13

   Christmas-Day.   13
   Feast of St. Stephen the Protomartyr.   17
   Feast of St. John.   18
   Holy Innocents.   19
   Feast of the Circumcision.   19
   Epiphany.   21
   Feast of the Most Holy Name of Jesus. Second Sunday after Epiphany.   22
   Friday after Septuagesima Sunday. Prayer of Our Lord Jesus Christ on Mount Olivet.   24
   Friday after Sexagesima. The Passion of Our Lord Jesus Christ.   25
   Friday after Quinquagesima. The Most Holy Crown of Thorns.   26
   Sundays and Week-Days in Lent.   27
   Friday after the First Sunday in Lent. The Spear and Nails.   28
   Friday after the Second Sunday Lent. The Most Holy Winding-Sheet.   29
   Friday after the Third Sunday in Lent. The Most Holy Five Wounds.   30
   Friday after the Fourth Sunday in Lent. The Most Precious Blood.   31
   Passion-Sunday.   33
   The Compassion of the Blessed Virgin Mary. Friday after Passion-Sunday.   34
   Palm-Sunday.   38

Good-Friday.	39
Easter Sunday.	41
Ascension-Day.	44
Whit-Sunday.	46
Trinity-Sunday. Morning.	50
Evening.	51
Corpus Christi.	51
Feast of the Most Sacred Heart of Jesus. Friday After the Octave of Corpus Christi.	58
Purification of the B. Virgin Mary.	60
Feast of St. Joseph.	61
Hymn to St. Joseph.	63
The Patronage of St. Joseph. Third Sunday after Easter.	64
Annunciation of the Blessed Virgin Mary.	65
Feast of St. Michael.	66
The Blessed VIrgin Mary the Help of Christians.	67
SS. Peter and Paul, Apostles.	68
Feast of St. John the Baptist.	69
Visitation of the Blessed Virgin Mary.	70
Feast of St. Anne, Mother of the Blessed Virgin Mary.	71
Feast of the Transfiguration.	72
Assumption of the Blessed Virgin Mary.	73
St. Rose of Lima.	74
Feast of the Nativity of the Blessed Virgin Mary.	75
Exaltation of the Holy Cross.	76
Seven Dolors of the Blessed Virgin Mary. Sunday After the Octave of the Nativity.	79
Feast of the Most Holy Guardian Angels.	80
Maternity of the Blessed Virgin Mary.	81
Purity of the Blessed Virgin Mary.	82
All Saints' Day.	83
Immaculate Conception of the Blessed Virgin Mary.	84
At Matins.	84

At Prime.	85
At Terce.	85
At Sext.	86
At None.	87
At Vespers.	87
At Compline.	88
The Commendation.	89
The Immaculate Conception.	89
Evening Hymn to the Blessed Virgin Mary.	91
Hymn for the Feasts of Apostles.	93
For the Feasts of Apostles and Evangelists.	94
For the Feasts of Martyrs.	95
For the Feasts of Confessors.	95
For the Feasts of Virgins.	97
Hymns at the Benediction of the Blessed Sacrament.	98
Jesus Our Redeemer.	103
The Day of Judgment.	104
HYMNS FOR PARTICULAR OCCASIONS OF DEVOTION.	107
HYMNS FOR COMMUNION.	107
Hymn of St. Francis Xavier.	107
My God and My All.	107
Holy Communion.	108
After Communion.	108
First Communion. Hymn of St. Bernard.	109
Longing for Christ.	110
HYMNS FOR CONFESSION.	111
The Sinner's Prayer.	111
After Confession	112
HYMNS FOR CONFIRMATION.	114
Offering.	114
HYMNS OF THE LITANY OF OUR LADY.	115
Lady Of Loretto.	115
Rosa Mystica.	116

Turris Eburnea.	117
Foederis Arca.	118
Janua Coeli.	119
Stella Matutina!	121
Domus Aurea.	122
All Saints!	123
Month of May. Pious Aspirations to the Mother of God, for Every Day in the Month.	125
Christmas Vesper Hymn.	128
HYMN BEFORE PRAYER, SERMON, CATECISM, ETC.	129
For Aid in Prayer. Another Hymn before Prayer, etc.	130
HYMN BEFORE SINGING.	131
HYMN BEFORE FAMILY PRAYER.	131
Our Great Protector.	132
Children of the Heavenly King.	133
Praises to the Lord.	134
Child's Prayer.	134
St. Vincent of Paul.	135
Hymn to St. Aloysius Gonzaga.	136
Hymn to St. Stanislaus Kotska.	138
Hymn to St. Cecilia.	139
Hymn to St. Francis Xavier.	140
Hymn to Our Blessed Lady, for the Souls in Purgatory.	140
HYMN TO MY GUARDIAN ANGEL.	142
For Children.	142
For a Happy Death.	144
The Most Holy Trinity.	145
The Infant Jesus	146
Jesus Crucified.	148
The Ascension.	150
The Mission of the Holy Ghost.	153
The Descent of the Holy Ghost.	155
To Our Blessed Lady.	158

The Assumption.	159
The Creation of the Angels.	160
Faith of Our Fathers.	162
The Right Must Win.	162
True Love.	165
Perfection.	168
The Eternal Father.	170
Jesus Risen.	172
The Apparition of Jesus to Our Blessed Lady.	173
Conversion.	175
In Praise of the Holy Cross.	177
Life, Passion, and Merits of Christ.	181
Part I.	181
Part II.	182
Part III.	183
PRAYER ON GOING TO SLEEP.	185
Prayer Before a Picture of Our Blessed Lady.	185
Prayer on Rising in the Morning.	185
Prayer on Going to Sleep.	186
Prayer to a Guardian Angel.	186
DOXOLOGY.	187

HYMNS FOR WEEK-DAYS AND SUNDAYS, WHEN NOT OTHERWISE APPOINTED.

MORNING HYMNS.

Somno reflctis artubus.

UR limbs with tranquil sleep refresh'd,
    Lightly from bed we spring;
Father supreme! to us be nigh,
    While to thy praise we sing.

Thy love be first in every heart,
    Thy name on every tongue;
Whatever we this day may do,
    May it in Thee be done.

Soon will the morning star arise,
    And chase the dusk away;
Whatever guilt has come with night,
    May it depart with day.

Cut off in us, Almighty Lord,
    All that may lead to shame;
So with pure hearts may we in bliss
    Thine endless praise proclaim.

Father of mercies! hear our cry;
    Hear us, coequal Son!
Who reignest with the Holy Ghost
    While ceaseless ages run.

Jam lucis orto sidere.

Now doth the sun ascend the sky,
 And wake creation with its ray;
Keep us from sin, O Lord most high!
 Through all the actions of the day.

Curb Thou for us th' unruly tongue;
 Teach us the way of peace to prize;
And close our eyes against the throng
 Of earth's absorbing vanities.

Oh, may our hearts be pure within!
 No cherish'd madness vex the soul!
May abstinence the flesh restrain,
 And its rebellious pride control.

So when the evening stars appear,
 And in their train the darkness bring,
May we, O Lord, with conscience clear,
 Our praise to thy pure glory sing.

To God the Father glory be,
 And to his sole-begotten Son;
The same, O Holy Ghost! to Thee,
 While everlasting ages run.

Lux ecce surgit aurea.

Now with the rising golden dawn,
 Let us, the children of the day,
Cast off the darkness which so long
 Has led our guilty souls astray.

Oh, may the morn so pure, so clear,
    Its own sweet calm in us instil;
A guileless mind, a heart sincere,
    Simplicity of word and will:

And ever, as the day glides by,
    May we the busy senses rein;
Keep guard upon the hand and eye,
    Nor let the body suffer stain.

For all day long, on Heaven's high tower,
    There stands a Sentinel, who spies
Our every action, hour by hour,
    From early dawn till daylight dies.

To God the Father glory be,
    And to his sole-begotten Son;
The same, O Holy Ghost! to Thee,
    While everlasting ages run.

SUNDAY MORNING.

Ad templa nos rursus vocat.

Again the Sunday morn
  Calls us to prayer and praise;
Waking our hearts to gratitude
  With its enlivening rays.

      But Christ yet brighter shone,
        Quenching the morning beam;
      When triumphing from death He rose,
        And raised us up with Him.

When first the world sprang forth,
   In majesty array'd,
And bathed in streams of purest light;
   What power was there display'd!

      But oh, what love! — when Christ,
         For our transgressions slain,
      Was by th' Eternal Father raised
         For us to life again.

His new-created world
   The mighty Maker view'd,
With thousand lovely tints adorn'd;
   And straight pronounced it good.

      But oh! much more He joy'd
         That self-same world to see,
      Wash'd in the Lamb's all-saving Blood,
         From its impurity.

Nature each day renews
   Her beauty evermore;
Whence to God's hidden Majesty,
   The soul is taught to soar.

      But Christ the Light of all,
         The Father's image blest,
      Gives us to see our God Himself
         In Flesh made manifest.

Blest Trinity! vouchsafe
   That to thy guidance true,
What Thou forbiddest, we may shun;
   What Thou commandest, do.

EVENING HYMNS.

Te tucis ante terminum.

1 Now with the fast-departing light,
    Maker of all! we ask of Thee,
Of thy great mercy, through the night,
    Our guardian and defence to be.

2 Far off let idle visions fly;
    No phantom of the night molest;
Curb Thou our raging enemy,
    That we in chaste repose may rest.

3 Father of mercies! hear our cry;
    Hear us, O sole-begotten Son!
Who with the Holy Ghost most high,
    Reignest while endless ages run.

    1 Te lucis ante terminum,
      Rerum Creator poscimus;
      Ut pro tua clementia,
      Sis praesul et custodia.

    2 Procul recedant somnia,
      Et noctium phantasmata;
      Hostemque nostrum comprime,
      Ne polluantur corpora.

    3 Praesta, Pater piisime,
      Patrique compar Unice,
      Cum Spiritu Paraclito
      Regnans per omne saeculum.

Lucis Creator Optima.

1 O BLEST Creator of the light!
    Who dost the dawn from darkness bring;
And framing Nature's depth and height,
    Didst with the new-born light begin;

2 Who gently blending eve with morn,
    And morn with eve, didst call them day: —
Thick flows the flood of darkness down;
    Oh, hear us as we weep and pray!

3 Keep Thou our souls from schemes of crime;
    Nor guilt remorseful let them know;
Nor, thinking but on things of time,
    Into eternal darkness go.

4 Teach us to knock at Heaven's high door;
    Teach us the prize of life to win
Teach us all evil to abhor,
    And purify ourselves within.

5 Father of mercies! hear our cry!
    Hear us, O sole-begotten Son!
Who, with the Holy Ghost most high,
    Reignest while endless ages run.

    1 Lucis Creator optime,
       Lucem dierum proferens,
       Primordiis lucis novae
       Mundi parans originem:

    2 Qui mane junctum vesperi
       Diem vocari praecipis;
       Illabitur tetrum chaos,
       Audi preces cum fletibus.

3 Ne mens gravata crimine,
   Vitae sit exul munere,
   Dum nil perenne cogitat,
   Seseque culpis illigat.

4 Coeleste pulset ostium:
   Vitale tollat praemium:
   Vitemus omne noxium:
   Purgemus omne pessimum.

5 Praesta, Pater piissime,
   Patrique compar Unice,
   Cum Spiritu Paraclito
   Regnans per omne saeculum.

Rerum Deus tenax vigor.

O THOU true life of all that live!
    Who dost, unmoved, all motion sway;
Who dost the morn and evening give,
    And through its changes guide the day:

Thy light upon our evening pour, —
    So may our souls no sunset see;
But death to us an open door
    To an eternal morning be.

Father of mercies! hear our cry
    Hear us, O sole-begotten Son!
Who, with the Holy Ghost most high,
    Reignest while endless ages run.

ANTIPHONS OF THE BLESSED VIRGIN. FROM THE FIRST SUNDAY IN ADVENT TO THE FEAST OF THE PURIFICATION.

Alma Redemptoris Mater.

MOTHER of Christ! hear thou thy people's cry.
Star of the deep, and Portal of the sky!
Mother of Him who thee from nothing made!
Sinking we strive, and call to thee for aid:
Oh, by that joy which Gabriel brought to thee,
Thou Virgin first and last, let us thy mercy see.

ALMA Redemptoris Mater, quae pervia coeli,
Porta manes, et stella maris, succurre cadenti.
Surgere qui curat, populo: tu quae genuisti,
Natura mirante, tuum sanctum Genitorem,
Virgo prius ac posterius, Gabrielis ab ore,
Sumens illud Ave, peccatorum miserere.

FROM THE PURIFICATION OF THE BLESSED VIRGIN TO PALM SUNDAY.

Ave Regina coelorum.

HAIL, O Queen of Heaven enthroned!
Hail, by angels Mistress own'd!
Root of Jesse! Gate of morn!
Whence the world's true Light was born:
Glorious Virgin, joy to thee,
Loveliest whom in Heaven they see:
Fairest thou where all are fair!
Plead with Christ our sins to spare.

Ave Regina coelorum,
Ave Domina Angelorum

> Salve radix, salve porta,
> Ex qua mundo lux est orta.
> Gaude Virgo gloriosa,
> Super omnes speciosa:
> Vale O valde decora,
> Et pro nobis Christum exora.

FROM EASTER SUNDAY TO WHITSUNDAY.

Regina coeli laetare.

JOY to thee, O Queen of Heaven! Alleluia.
    He whom thou wast meet to bear; Alleluia.
As He promised, hath arisen; Alleluia.
    Pour for us to Him thy prayer; Alleluia.

> REGINA coeli laetare, Alleluia.
> Quia quem meruisti portare, Alleluia.
> Resurrexit sicut dixit, Alleluia.
> Ora pro nobis Deum, Alleluia.

FROM TRINITY SUNDAY TO THE LAST SUNDAY AFTER PENTECOST.

Salve Regina, Mater misericordiae.

MOTHER of mercy, hail, O gentle Queen!
Our life, our sweetness, and our hope, all hail!
    Children of Eve,
To thee we cry from our sad banishment;
    To thee we send our sighs,
Weeping and mourning in this tearful vale.
    Come, then, our Advocate;
Oh, turn on us those pitying eyes of thine:
    And, our long exile past,

　　　　Show us at last
Jesus, of thy pure womb the fruit divine.
　　　O Virgin Mary, Mother blest!
　　　O sweetest, gentlest, holiest!

SALVE regina, mater misericordiae,
vita, dulcedo, et spes nostra, salve.
Ad te clamamus exules filii Hevae.
Ad te suspiramus gementes et flentes in hac
lacrymarum valle.
Eja ergo advocata nostra, illos tuos misericordes
oculos ad nos converte.
Et Jesum, benedictum fructum ventris tui,
nobis post hoc exilium ostende.
O Clemens, O pia, O dulcis Virgo Maria.

SUNDAYS AND WEEK-DAYS IN ADVENT.

Creator alme sideram.

MAKER of Heaven, eternal light
　　Of all who in thy name believe!
Jesu! Redeemer of mankind!
　　An ear to thy poor suppliants give.

When man was sunk in sin and death,
　　Lost in the depth of Satan's snare,
Love brought Thee down to cure our ills,
　　By taking of those ills a share.

Thou, for the sake of guilty men,
　　Causing thine own pure blood to flow,
Didst issue from thy Virgin shrine,
　　And to the Cross a Victim go.
So great the glory of thy might,

If we but chance thy name to sound,
   At once all Heaven and Hell unite
      In bending low with awe profound.

Great Judge of all! in that last day,
      When friends shall fail, and foes combine,
Be present then with us, we pray,
      To guard us with thy arm divine.

To God the Father, and the Son,
      All praise and power and glory be
With Thee, O holy Comforter!
      Henceforth through all eternity.

[Within the Octave of the Feast of the Conception.]
O Jesu! born of Virgin bright,
      Immortal glory be to Thee;
Praise to the Father infinite,
      And Holy Ghost eternally.

En clara vox redarguit.

HARK! an awful voice is sounding;
      "Christ is nigh!" it seems to say;
"Cast away the dreams of darkness,
      O ye children of the day!"

Startled at the solemn warning,
      Let the earth-bound soul arise;
Christ her Sun, all sloth dispelling,
      Shines upon the morning skies.

Lo! the Lamb so long expected,
      Comes with pardon down from Heaven;
Let us haste, with tears of sorrow,
      One and all to be forgiven.

So, when next He comes with glory,
    Wrapping all the earth in fear,
May He then as our Defender
    On the clouds of Heaven appear.

Honor, glory, virtue, merit,
    To the Father and the Son,
With the everlasting Spirit,
    While eternal ages run.

HYMNS FOR THE PRINCIPAL HOLY DAYS AND SAINTS' DAYS.

CHRISTMAS-DAY.

Jesu Redemptor omnium.

JESU, Redeemer of the world,
    Who, ere the earliest dawn of light,
Wast from eternal ages born,
    Immense in glory as in might;

Immortal Hope of all mankind!
    In whom the Father's face we see;
Hear Thou the prayers thy people pour
    This day throughout the world to Thee.

Remember, O Creator Lord!
    That in the Virgin's sacred womb
Thou wast conceived, and of her flesh
    Didst our mortality assume.

This ever-blest recurring day
    Its witness bears, that all alone,
From thy own Father's bosom forth,
    To save the world Thou camest down.

O Day! to which the seas and sky,
    And earth and Heaven glad welcome sing;
O Day! which heal'd our misery,
    And brought on earth salvation's King.

We too, O Lord, who have been cleansed
    In thy own fount of blood divine,

Offer the tribute of sweet song,
    On this blest natal day of thine.

O Jesu! born of Virgin bright,
    Immortal glory be to Thee
Praise to the Father infinite,
    And Holy Ghost eternally.

Adeste fideles.

1 OH, come! all ye faithful!
      Triumphantly sing!
   Come, see in the Manger
      The Angels' dread King!
   To Bethlehem hasten!
      With joyful accord;
   Oh, hasten! Oh, hasten!
      To worship the Lord.

2 True Son of the Father!
      He comes from the skies;
   The womb of the Virgin
      He doth not despise;
   To Bethlehem hasten, &c., *as above.*

3 Hark! to the Angels!
      All singing in Heaven,
   "To God in the highest
      All glory be given."
   To Bethlehem hasten, &c.

4 To Thee, then, O Jesu!
      This day of thy birth
   Be glory and honor
      Through Heaven and earth;

True Godhead Incarnate!
Omnipotent Word!
Oh, hasten! oh, hasten!
To worship the Lord.

1 ADESTE, fideles,
Laeti triumphantes;
Venite, venite in Bethlehem;
Natum videte
Regem angelorum:
Venite adoremus,
Venite adoremus,
Venite adoremus Dominum.

2 Deum de Deo,
Lumen de Lumine,
Gestant puellae viscera:
Deum verum,
Genitum, non factum:
Venite adoremus, &c.

3 Cantet nunc Io
Chorus Angelorum;
Cantet nunc aula coelestium,
Gloria in excelsis Deo:
Venite adoremus, &c.

4 Ergo qui natus
Die hodierna,
Jesu, tibi sit gloria:
Patris aeterni
Verbum caro factum:
Venite adoremus, &c.

[*For singing.*]

1 YE faithful, approach ye,
   Joyfully triumphing
Oh, come ye, oh, come ye, to Bethlehem;
   Come, and behold ye
   Born the King of angels:
   Oh, come, let us worship,
   Oh, come, let us worship,
Oh, come, let us worship Christ the Lord.

2 True God of God,
   True Light of Light,
Lo, He disdains not the Virgin's womb;
   Very God,
   Begotten, not created:
Oh, come, let us worship, &c.

3 Sing Halleluiah,
   Let the courts of Heaven
Ring with the Angel-chorus, —
   Praise the Lord,
   Glory to God in the highest
Oh, come, let us worship, &c.

4 Yea, Lord, we greet Thee,
   Born this happy morning;
Jesu, to Thee be glory given:
   Word of the Father
   In our flesh appearing:
Oh, come, let us worship, &c.

FEAST OF ST. STEPHEN THE PROTOMARTYR.

December 26.

O qui tuo dux Martyrum.

O CAPTAIN of the Martyr Host!
    O peerless in renown!
Not from the fading flowers of earth
    Weave we for thee a crown.

The stones that smote thee, in thy blood
    Made glorious and divine,
All in a halo heavenly bright
    About thy temples shine.

The scars upon thy sacred brow
    Throw beams of glory round;
The splendors of thy bruised face
    The very sun confound.

Oh, earliest Victim sacrificed
    To thy dear Victim Lord!
Oh, earliest witness to the Faith
    Of thy Incarnate God!

Thou to the heavenly Canaan first
    Through the Red Sea didst go,
And to the Martyrs' countless host,
    Their path of glory show.

Erewhile a servant of the poor, —
    Now at the Lamb's high Feast,
In blood-empurpled robe array'd,
    A welcome nuptial guest!

To Jesus, born of Virgin bright,
    Praise with the Father be;
Praise to the Spirit Paraclete,
    Through all eternity.

FEAST OF ST. JOHN.

December 27.

Quæ dixit, egit, pertulit.

THE life which God's Incarnate Word
    Lived here below with men,
Three blest Evangelists record,
    With Heaven-inspired pen.

John penetrates on eagle wing
    The Father's dread abode;
And shows the mystery wherein
    The Word subsists with God.

Pure Saint! upon his Saviour's breast
    Invited to recline,
'Twas thence he drew, in moments blest,
    His knowledge all divine:

There, too, with that angelic love
    Did he his bosom fill,
Which, once enkindled from above,
    Breathes in his pages still.

Oh, dear to Christ! — to thee upon
    His Cross, of all bereft,
Thou virgin soul! the Virgin Son
    His Virgin Mother left.

To Jesus, born of Virgin bright,
    Praise with the Father be;
Praise to the Spirit Paraclete,
    Through all eternity.

HOLY INNOCENTS.

December 28.

Salvete flares martyrum.

LOVELY flowers of martyrs, hail!
    Smitten by the tyrant foe —
On life's threshold, — as the gale
    Strews the roses ere they blow.

First to die for Christ, sweet lambs!
    At the very altar ye,
With your fatal crowns and palms,
    Sport in your simplicity.

Honor, glory, virtue, merit,
    Be to Thee, O Virgin's Son!
With the Father, and the Spirit,
    While eternal ages run.

FEAST OF THE CIRCUMCISION.

January 1.

A solis ortus cardine.

FROM the far blazing gate of morn
    To earth's remotest shore,
Let every tongue confess to Him
    Whom holy Mary bore.

Lo! the great Maker of the world,
    Lord of eternal years,
To save his creatures, veil'd beneath
    A creature's form appears.

A spotless maiden's virgin breast
    With heavenly grace he fills;
In her pure womb He is conceived,
    And there in secret dwells.

That bosom, Chastity's sweet home,
    Becomes, oh, blest reward!
The shrine of Heaven's immortal King,
    The temple of the Lord.

And Mary bears the babe, foretold
    By an archangel's voice;
Whose presence made the Baptist leap,
    And in the womb rejoice.

A manger scantly strewn with hay
    Becomes th' Eternal's bed;
And He, who feeds each smallest bird,
    Himself with milk is fed.

Straightway with joy the Heavens are fill'd,
    The hosts angelic sing;
And shepherds hasten to adore
    Their Shepherd and their King.

Praise to the Father! praise to Thee,
    Thou Virgin's holy Son!
Praise to the Spirit Paraclete,
    While endless ages run.

EPIPHANY.

January 6.

O sola magnarum urbium.

BETHLEHEM! of noblest cities
    None can once with thee compare;
Thou alone the Lord from Heaven
    Didst for us Incarnate bear.

Fairer than the sun at morning
    Was the star that told his birth;
To the lands their God announcing,
    Hid beneath a form of earth.

By its lambent beauty guided,
    See, the Eastern kings appear;
See them bend, their gifts to offer,
    Gifts of incense, gold, and myrrh.

Offerings of mystic meaning!—
    Incense doth the God disclose;
Gold a royal child proclaimeth;
    Myrrh a future tomb foreshows.

Holy Jesu! in thy brightness
    To the Gentile world display'd!
With the Father, and the Spirit,
    Endless praise to Thee be paid.

FEAST OF THE MOST HOLY NAME OF JESUS.
SECOND SUNDAY AFTER EPIPHANY.

Jesu dulcis memoria.

JESU! the very thought of Thee
    With sweetness fills my breast,
But sweeter far thy face to see,
    And in thy presence rest.

Nor voice can sing, nor heart can frame,
    Nor can the memory find,
A sweeter sound than thy blest name,
    O Saviour of mankind!

O hope of every contrite heart,
    O joy of all the meek,
To those who fall, how kind Thou art,
    How good to those who seek!

But what to those who find? ah! this
    Nor tongue nor pen can show;
The love of Jesus, what it is
    None but his loved ones know.

Jesu! our only joy be Thou,
    As Thou our prize wilt be
Jesu! be Thou our glory now,
    And through eternity.

[Jesu Rex admirabilis.]

O JESU! King most wonderful!
    Thou Conqueror renown'd!
Thou Sweetness most ineffable!
    In whom all joys are found!

When once Thou visitest the heart,
    Then truth begins to shine;
Then earthly vanities depart;
    Then kindles love divine.

O Jesu! Light of all below!
    Thou Fount of life and fire!
Surpassing all the joys we know,
    All that we can desire:

May every heart confess thy name,
    And ever Thee adore;
And seeking Thee, itself inflame
    To seek Thee more and more.

Thee may our tongues forever bless;
    Thee may we love alone;
And ever in our lives express
    The image of thine own.

[Jesu decus angelicum.]

O JESU! Thou the beauty art
    Of angel worlds above;
Thy name is music to the heart,
    Enchanting it with love.

Celestial sweetness unalloy'd!
    Who eat Thee hunger still;
Who drink of Thee still feel a void,
    Which naught but Thou can fill.

O my sweet Jesu! hear the sighs
    Which unto Thee I send;
To Thee mine inmost spirit cries,
    My being's hope and end!

Stay with us, Lord, and with thy light
    Illume the soul's abyss;
Scatter the darkness of our night,
    And fill the world with bliss.

O Jesu! spotless Virgin flower!
    Our love and joy! to Thee
Be praise, beatitude, and power,
    Through all eternity.

FRIDAY AFTER SEPTUAGESIMA SUNDAY.
PRAYER OF OUR LORD JESUS CHRIST ON MOUNT OLIVET.

Aspice at Verbum Patris a supernis.

SEE from on high, array'd in truth and grace,
    The Father's Word descend!
Burning to heal the wounds of Adam's race,
    And our long evil s end!

Pitying the miseries which with the Fall
    In Paradise began,
Prostrate upon the earth, the Lord of all
    Entreats for ruin'd man.

Oh, bitter then was our Redeemer's lot,
    While whelm'd in griefs unknown:
"Father," He cries, "remove this cup; yet not
    My will, but thine be done:"

While, a dread anguish pressing down his heart,
    He faints upon the ground;
And from each bursting pore the blood-drops start,
    Moistening the earth around.

But quickly, from high Heaven, an angel came,
    To soothe the Saviour's woes
And, strength returning to his languid frame,
    Up from the earth He rose.

Praise to the Father; praise, O Son! To Thee,
    To whom a name is given
Above all names; praise to the Spirit be,
    From all in earth and Heaven.

FRIDAY AFTER SEXAGESIMA.
THE PASSION OF OUR LORD JESUS CHRIST.

Saevo dolorum turbine.

O'ERWHELM'D in depths of woe,
    Upon the tree of scorn
Hangs the Redeemer of mankind,
    With racking anguish torn.

See! how the nails those hands
    And feet so tender rend;
See! down his face, and neck, and breast,
    His sacred blood descend.

Hark! with what awful cry
    His Spirit takes its flight;
That cry, it pierced his Mother's heart,
    And whelm'd her soul in night.

Earth hears, and to its base
    Rocks wildly to and fro;
Tombs burst; seas, rivers, mountains quake;
    The veil is rent in two.

The sun withdraws his light;
    The midday heavens grow pale;
The moon, the stars, the universe,
    Their Maker's death bewail.

Shall man alone be mute?
    Come, youth! and hoary hairs!
Come, rich and poor! come, all mankind!
    And bathe those feet in tears.

Come! fall before His Cross,
    Who shed for us his blood!
Who died the victim of pure love,
    To make us sons of God.

Jesu! all praise to Thee,
    Our joy and endless rest!
Be Thou our guide while pilgrims here,
    Our crown amid the blest.

FRIDAY AFTER QUINQUAGESIMA.
THE MOST HOLY CROWN OF THORNS.

Exite Sion filiae.

DAUGHTERS of Sion! royal maids!
    Come forth to see the crown,
Which Sion's self, with cruel hands,
    Hath woven for her Son.

See! how amid his gory locks
    The jagged thorns appear;
See! how his pallid countenance
    Foretells that death is near.

Oh, savage was the earth that bore
    Those thorns so sharp and long!
Savage the hand that gather'd them
    To work this deadly wrong!

But now that Christ's immortal Blood
    Hath tinged them with its dye,
Fairer than roses they appear,
    Or palms of victory.

Jesu! the thorns which pierced thy brow
    Sprang from the seed of sin;
Pluck ours, we pray Thee, from our hearts,
    And plant thine own therein.

Praise, honor, to the Father be,
    Praise to his only Son;
Praise to the blessed Paraclete,
    While endless ages run.

SUNDAYS AND WEEK-DAYS IN LENT.

Audi benigne Conditor.

THOU loving Maker of mankind,
    Before thy throne we pray and weep;
Oh, strengthen us with grace divine,
    Duly this sacred Lent to keep.

Searcher of hearts! Thou dost our ills
    Discern, and all our weakness know;
Again to Thee with tears we turn;
    Again to us thy mercy show.

Much have we sinn'd but we confess
    Our guilt, and all our faults deplore:

Oh, for the praise of thy great Name,
    Our fainting souls to health restore!

And grant us, while by fasts we strive
    This mortal body to control,
To fast from all the food of sin,
    And so to purify the soul.

Hear us, O Trinity thrice blest!
    Sole Unity! to Thee we cry:
Vouchsafe us from these fasts below
    To reap immortal fruit on high.

FRIDAY AFTER THE FIRST SUNDAY IN LENT.
THE SPEAR AND NAILS.

Tinctam ergo Christi sanguine.

OH, turn those blessed points, all bathed
    In Jesu's blood, on me;
Mine were the sins that wrought his death,
    Mine be the penalty.

Pierce through my feet, my hands, my heart;
    So may some drop distil
Of Blood divine, into my soul,
    And all its evils heal.

So shall my feet be slow to sin,
    Harmless my hands shall be;
So from my wounded heart shall each
    Forbidden passion flee.

Thee, Jesu, pierced with Nails and Spear.
    Let every knee adore;

With Thee, O Father, and with Thee,
    O Spirit, evermore.

FRIDAY AFTER THE SECOND SUNDAY LENT.
THE MOST HOLY WINDING-SHEET.

Mysterium mirabile.

THIS day the wondrous mystery
    Is set before our eyes,
Of Jesus stretch'd upon the Cross
    In dying agonies.

Oh, deed of love! the Prince becomes
    A Victim for his slave;
The sinner an acquittal finds,
    The innocent a grave.

Whereof, in many a gory stain,
    The traces still are found
On yonder Winding-Sheet, which wrapp'd
    The sacred body round.

Hail, trophies of our valiant Chief!
    Hail, proofs of triumph won
Over the World, and Hell, and Death
    By God's eternal Son!

Be these the colors under which
    From this time forth we fight,
Against the depths of Satan's guile,
    And all the powers of night.

So, dead to our old life, may we
    A better life begin;

And through the Cross of Christ at length
    His Heavenly Crown attain.

Father of mercies! hear our cry;
    Hear us, coequal Son!
Who reignest with the Holy Ghost
    While ceaseless ages run.

FRIDAY AFTER THE THIRD SUNDAY IN LENT.
THE MOST HOLY FIVE WOUNDS.

Pange lingua gloriosi.

SING, my tongue, the Saviour's glory:
    Tell his triumph far and wide;
Tell aloud the famous story
    Of his Body crucified;
How upon the Cross a Victim,
    Vanquishing in death, He died.

Lo, with gall his thirst He quenches!
    See the thorns upon his brow!
Nails his tender flesh are rending!
    See, his side is open'd now!
Whence, to cleanse the whole creation,
    Streams of blood and water flow.

Blessing, honor everlasting,
    To th' immortal Deity;
To the Father, Son, and Spirit,
    Equal praises ever be:
Glory through the earth and Heaven
    To Trinity in Unity.

FRIDAY AFTER THE FOURTH SUNDAY IN LENT. THE MOST PRECIOUS BLOOD.

Salvete Christi vulnera.

HAIL, wounds! which through eternal years
    The love of Jesus Show;
Hail, wounds! from whence encrimson'd rills
    Of blood forever flow.

More precious than the gems of Ind,
    Than all the stars more fair;
Nor honeycomb, nor fragrant rose,
    Can once with you compare.

Through you is opened to our souls
    A refuge safe and calm,
Whither no raging enemy
    Can reach to work us harm.

What countless stripes did Christ receive
    Naked in Pilate's hall!
From his torn flesh what streams of blood
    Did all around him fall!

How doth th' ensanguined thorny crown
    That beauteous brow transpierce!
How doth the nails those hands and feet
    Contract with tortures fierce!

He bows his head, and forth at last
    His loving spirit soars;
Yet even after death his heart
    For us its tribute pours.

Beneath the wine-press of God's wrath
    His Blood for us He drains;

Till for Himself, O wondrous love!
    No single drop remains.

Oh, come all ye in whom are fix'd
    The deadly stains of sin!
Come! wash in this all-saving Blood,
    And ye shall be made clean.

Praise Him, who with the Father sits
    Enthroned upon the skies;
Whose Blood redeems our souls from guilt,
    Whose Spirit sanctifies.

Viva, viva, Gesù.[1]

HAIL, Jesus, hail who for my sake
Sweet Blood from Mary's veins didst take,
    And Shed it all for me;
Oh, blessed be my Saviour's Blood,
My life, my light, my only good,
    To all eternity.

To endless ages let us praise
The precious Blood whose price could raise
    The world from wrath and sin;
Whose streams our inward thirst appease,
And heal the sinner's worst disease,
    If he but bathe therein.

O sweetest Blood! that can implore
Pardon of God, and heaven restore,
    The heaven that sin had lost;
While Abel's blood for vengeance pleads,

---

[1] From the "Raccolta delle Indulgenze," &c.

What Jesus shed still intercedes
    For those who wrong Him most.

Oh, to be sprinkled from the wells
Of Christ's own sacred Blood, excels
    Earth's best and highest bliss:
The ministers of wrath divine
Hurt not the happy hearts that shine
    With those red drops of his!

Ah! there is joy amid the Saints,
And hell's despairing courage faints
    When this sweet song we raise:
Oh, louder then, and louder still,
Earth with one mighty chorus fill,
    The precious Blood to praise!

PASSION-SUNDAY.

Vexilla Regis prodeunt.

FORTH comes the Standard of the King:
    All hail, thou Mystery adored!
Hail, Cross! on which the Life Himself
    Died, and by death our life restored:

On which our Saviour's holy side,
    Rent open with a cruel spear,
Of blood and water pour'd a stream,
    To wash us from defilement clear.

O sacred Wood! in thee fulfill'd
    Was holy David's truthful lay;
Which told the world that from a Tree
    The Lord should all the nations sway.

Most royally empurpled o'er,
    How beauteously thy stem doth shine!
How glorious was its lot to touch
    Those limbs so holy and divine!

Thrice blest, upon whose arms outstretch'd
    The Saviour of the world reclined;
Balance sublime! upon whose beam
    Was weigh'd the ransom of mankind.

Hail, Cross! thou only hope of man,
    Hail on this holy Passion-day!
To saints increase the grace they have;
    From sinners purge their guilt away.

Salvation's spring, blest Trinity,
    Be praise to Thee through earth and skies:
Thou through the Cross the victory
    Dost give; oh, also give the prize!

THE COMPASSION OF THE BLESSED VIRGIN MARY. FRIDAY AFTER PASSION-SUNDAY.

Stabat Mater dolorosa.

1 AT the Cross her station keeping,
    Stood the mournful Mother weeping,
      Close to Jesus to the last:
    Through her heart, his sorrow sharing,
    All his bitter anguish bearing,
      Now at length the sword had pass'd.

2 Oh, how sad and sore distress'd
    Was that Mother highly blest
      Of the sole-begotten One!

Christ above in torment hangs:
She beneath beholds the pangs
   Of her dying glorious Son.

3 Is there one who would not weep,
    Whelm'd in miseries so deep
       Christ's dear Mother to behold!
    Can the human heart refrain
    From partaking in her pain,
       In that Mother's pain untold?

4 Bruised, derided, cursed, defiled,
    She beheld her tender Child
       All with bloody scourges rent;
    For the sins of his own nation,
    Saw Him hang in desolation,
       Till his Spirit forth He sent.

5 O then Mother! fount of love!
    Touch my spirit from above,
       Make my heart with thine accord;
    Make me feel as thou hast felt;
    Make my soul to glow and melt
       With the love of Christ my Lord.

[Sancta Mater, istud agas.]

6 HOLY Mother! pierce me through;
    In my heart each wound renew
       Of my Saviour crucified:
    Let me share with thee his pain
    Who for all my sins was slain,
       Who for me in torments died.

7 Let me mingle tears with thee,
    Mourning Him who mourn'd for me,
       All the days that I may live:

By the Cross with thee to stay;
There with thee to weep and pray;
   Is all I ask of thee to give.

[Virgo virginum praeclara.]

8 VIRGIN of all virgins best!
Listen to my fond request:
   Let me share thy grief divine;
Let me, to my latest breath,
In my body bear the death
   Of that dying Son of thine.

9 Wounded with his every wound,
Steep my soul till it hath swoon'd
   In his very blood away;
Be to me, O Virgin, nigh,
Lest in flames I burn and die,
   In his awful Judgment day.

10   Christ, when Thou shalt, call me hence,
Be thy Mother my defence,
   Be thy Cross my victory;
While my body here decays,
May my soul thy goodness praise,
   Safe in Paradise with Thee.

  1   STABAT Mater dolorosa,
    Juxta crucem lacrymosa,
    Dum pendebat Filius;
    Cujus animam gementem,
    Contristatam et dolentem,
    Pertransivit gladius.

  2 O quam tristis et afflicta
    Fuit illa benedicta
    Mater Unigeniti!

Quae moerebat, et dolebat,
   Pia Mater dum videbat
   Nati poenas inclyti.

3 Quis est homo, qui non fleret,
   Matrem Christi si videret
   In tanto supplicio?
   Quis non posset contristari,
   Christi Matrem contemplari,
   Dolentem cum Filio?

4 Pro peccatis suae gentis,
   Vidit Jesum in tormentis,
   Et flagellis subditum.
   Vidit suum dulcem natum
   Moriendo desolatum,
   Dum emisit spiritum.

5 Eia Mater, fons amoris,
   Me sentire vim doloris,
   Fac ut tecum lugeam.
   Fac ut ardeat cor meum
   In amando Christum Deum,
   Ut sibi complaceam.

6 Sancta Mater, istud agas,
   Crucifixi fige plagas
   Cordi meo valide.
   Tui nati vulnerati,
   Tam dignati pro me pati,
   Poenas mecum divide.

7 Fac me tecum pie flere,
   Crucifixo condolere,
   Donec ego vixero.

Juxta crucem tecum stare,
  Et me tibi sociare,
  In planctu desidero.

8 Virgo virginum praeclara,
  Mihi jam non sis amara,
  Fac me tecum plangere.
  Fac ut portem Christi mortem,
  Passionis fac consortem,
  Et plagas recolere.

9 Fac me plagis vulnerari,
  Fac me cruce inebriari,
  Et cruore Filii:
  Flammis ne urar succensus,
  Per te Virgo sim defensus.
  In die judicii.

10 Christe, cum sit hinc exire,
   Da per Matrem me venire,
   Ad palmam victoriae.
   Quando corpus morietur,
   Fac ut animae donetur
   Paradisi gloria.

PALM-SUNDAY.

Gloria, laus, et honor.

GLORY and praise to Thee, Redeemer blest!
To whom their glad hosannas children pour'd
Hail, Israel's King! hail, David's Son confess'd!
Who comest in the name of Israel's Lord.

Thy praise in Heaven the Host angelic sings;
On earth mankind, with all created things.
["Glory and praise," &c. *as above, is repeated.*]

Thee once with palms the Jews went forth to meet,
Thee now with prayers and holy hymns we greet.
[Glory and praise, &c.]

Thee, on thy way to die, they crown'd with praise;
To Thee, now King on high, our song we raise.
[Glory and praise, &c.]

Thee their poor homage pleased, O gracious King!
Ours too accept, — the best that we can bring.
[Glory and praise, &c.]

GOOD-FRIDAY.

O Deus, ego amo Te.

[Hymn of St. Francis Xavier.]

MY God, I love Thee, not because
   I hope for Heaven thereby;
Nor because they, who love Thee not,
   Must burn eternally.

Thou, O my Jesus, Thou didst me
   Upon the Cross embrace;
For me didst bear the nails and spear
   And manifold disgrace;

And griefs and torments numberless;
   And sweat of agony;
E'en death itself — and all for one
   Who was thine enemy.

Then why, O blessed Jesu Christ!
    Should I not love Thee well;
Not for the sake of winning Heaven,
    Or of escaping Hell:

Not with the hope of gaining aught;
    Not seeking a reward;
But, as Thyself hast loved me,
    O ever-loving Lord?

E'en so I love Thee, and will love,
    And in thy praise will sing;
Solely because Thou art my God,
    And my eternal King.

Aspice infami Deus ipse ligno.

SEE! where in shame the God of glory hangs,
    All bathed in his own blood:
See! how the nails pierce with a thousand pangs
    Those hands so good.

Th' All Holy, as a minister of ill,
    Betwixt two thieves they place;
Oh, deed unjust! yet such the cruel will
    Of Israel's race.

Pale grows his face, and fix'd his languid eye;
    His wearied head He bends;
And rich in merits, forth with one loud cry
    His Spirit sends.

O heart more hard than iron! not to weep
    At this; thy sin it was
That wrought his death; of all these torments deep
    Thou art the cause.

Praise, honor, glory, be through endless time
    To th' everlasting God;
Who wiped away our deadly stains of crime
    In his own Blood.

EASTER SUNDAY.

Aurora coelum purpurat.

THE dawn was purpling o'er the sky;
    With alleluias rang the air;
Earth held a glorious jubilee;
    Hell gnash'd its teeth in fierce despair:

When our most valiant mighty King
    From death's abyss, in dread array,
Led the long-prison'd Fathers forth,
    Into the beam of life and day:

When He, whom stone, and seal, and guard,
    Had safely to the tomb consign'd,
Triumphant rose, and buried Death
    Deep in the grave He left behind.

"Calm all your grief, and still your tears,"
    Hark! the descending angel cries;
"For Christ is risen from the dead,
    And Death is slain, no more to rise."

O Jesu! from the death of sin
    Keep us, we pray; so shalt Thou be
The everlasting Paschal joy
    Of all the souls new born in Thee.

Now to the Father, and the Son
    Who rose from death, be glory given;

With Thee, O holy Comforter!
    Henceforth by all in earth and Heaven.

Ad regias agni dapes.

Now at the Lamb's high festival
    In robes of saintly white we sing,
Through the Red Sea in safety brought
    By Jesus our immortal King.

O Charity divine! his Blood
    He gives, to crown the royal feast:
His Flesh for us He immolates,
    Himself the Victim, Love the Priest.

And as the avenging Angel pass'd
    Of old the blood-besprinkled door;
As the cleft sea a passage gave,
    Then closed to whelm th' Egyptians o'er:

So Christ, our Paschal Sacrifice,
    Has brought us safe all perils through;
While for unleaven'd bread we need
    But heart sincere and purpose true.

Hail purest Victim Heaven could find,
    The powers of Hell to overthrow!
Who didst the chains of Death destroy;
    Who dost the prize of Life bestow.

Hail, victor Christ! hail, risen King!
    To Thee alone belongs the crown;
Who hast the heavenly gates unbarr'd,
    And dragg'd the Prince of darkness down.

O Jesu! from the death of sin
    Keep us, we pray; so shalt Thou be

The everlasting paschal joy
   Of all the souls new born in Thee.

Now to the Father, and the Son
   Who rose from death, be glory given;
With Thee, O holy Comforter,
   Henceforth by all in earth and Heaven.

O filii et filiae.

YE sons and daughters of the Lord!
The King of glory, King adored,
This day Himself from death restored.

All in the early morning gray,
Went holy women on their way,
To see the tomb where Jesus lay.

Of spices pure a precious store
In their pure hands those women bore,
To anoint the sacred Body o'er.

Then straightway one in white they see,
Who saith, "Ye seek the Lord; but He
Is risen, and gone to Galilee."

This told they Peter, told they John;
Who forthwith to the tomb are gone,
But Peter is by John outrun.

That self-same night, while out of fear
The doors were shut, the Lord most dear
To his Apostles did appear.

But Thomas, when of this he heard,
Was doubtful of his brethren's word;
Wherefore again there comes the Lord.

"Thomas, behold my side," saith He;
"My hands, my feet, my body see,
And doubt not, but believe in Me."

When Thomas saw that wounded side,
The truth no longer he denied;
"Thou art my Lord and God!" he cried.

Oh, blest are they who have not seen
Their Lord, and yet believe in Him!
Eternal life awaiteth them.

Now let us praise the Lord most high,
And strive his name to magnify
On this great day, through earth and sky:

Whose mercy ever runneth o'er;
Whom men and Angel Hosts adore;
To Him be glory evermore.

ASCENSION-DAY.

AEterne Rex altissime.

O THOU eternal King most high!
    Who didst the world redeem;
And conquering Death and Hell, receive
    A dignity supreme.

Thou, through the starry orbs this day,
    Didst to thy throne ascend;

Thenceforth to reign in sovereign power,
    And glory without end.

There, seated in thy majesty,
    To Thee submissive bow
The Heaven of Heavens, the spacious earth,
    The depths of Hell below.

With trembling there the angels see
    The changed estate of men;
The flesh which sinn'd by Flesh redeem'd;
    Man in the Godhead reign.

There, waiting for thy faithful souls,
    Be Thou to us, O Lord!
Our peerless joy while here we stay,
    In Heaven our great reward.

Renew our strength; our sins forgive;
    Our miseries efface;
And lift our souls aloft to Thee,
    By thy celestial grace.

So, when Thou shinest on the clouds,
    With thy angelic train,
May we be saved from vengeance due,
    And our lost crowns regain.

Glory to Jesus, who returns
    Triumphantly to Heaven;
Praise to the Father evermore,
    And Holy Ghost, be given.

WHIT-SUNDAY.

Jam Christus astra ascenderat.

    ABOVE the starry spheres,
      To where He was before,
Christ had gone up, so on from on high
      The Father's gift to pour:

    And now had fully come,
      On mystic cycle borne
Of seven times seven revolving days,
      The Pentecostal morn:

    When, as the Apostles knelt
      At the third hour in prayer,
A sudden rushing sound proclaim'd
      The God of glory near.

    Forthwith a tongue of fire
      Alights on every brow;—
Each breast receives the Father's light,
      The Word's enkindling glow.

    The Holy Ghost on all
      Is mightily outpour'd;
Who straight in divers tongues declare
      The wonders of the Lord.

    While strangers of all climes
      Flock round from far and near,
And, with amazement, each at once
      Their native accents hear.

    But Judah, faithless still,
      Denies the hand divine;

And madly jeers the Saints of Christ,
    As drunk with new-made wine.

Till Peter in the midst
    Stood up, and spake aloud;
And their perfidious falsity
    By Joel's witness show'd.

Praise to the Father be!
    Praise to the Son who rose!
Praise, Holy Paraclete, to Thee,
    While age on ages flows!

Veni Creator Spiritus.

1 COME, O Creator Spirit blest!
   And in our souls take up thy rest;
   Come, with thy grace and heavenly aid,
   To fill the hearts which Thou hast made.

2 Great Paraclete! to Thee we cry:
   O highest gift of God most high!
   O fount of life! O fire of love!
   And sweet Anointing from above!

3 Then in thy sevenfold gifts art known;
   Thee Finger of God's hand we own;
   The promise of the Father Thou!
   Who dost the tongue with power endow.

4 Kindle our senses from above,
   And make our hearts o'erflow with love;
   With patience firm, and virtue high,
   The weakness of our flesh supply.

5 Far from us drive the foe we dread,
   And grant us thy true peace instead;
   So shall we not, with Thee for guide,
   Turn from the path of life a side.

6 Oh, may thy grace on us bestow,
   The Father and the Son to know,
   And Thee through endless times confess'd
   Of Both th' eternal Spirit blest.

7 All glory while the ages run
   Be to the Father, and the Son
   Who rose from death; the same to Thee,
   O Holy Ghost, eternally.

    1 VENI, Creator Spiritus,
      Mentes tuorum visita,
      Imple superna gratia
      Quae tu creasti, pectora.

    2 Qui diceris Paraclitus,
      Altissimi donum Dei,
      Fons vivus, ignis, charitas,
      Et spiritalis unctio.

    3 Tu septiformis munere,
      Digitus Paternae dexterae,
      Tu rite promissum Patris,
      Sermone ditans guttura.

    4 Accende lumen sensibus:
      Infunde amorem cordibus:
      Infirma nostri corporis
      Virtute firmans perpeti.

5 Hostem repellas longius,
   Pacemque dones protinus:
   Ductore sic te praevio
   Vitemus omne noxium.

6 Per te seiamus da Patrem,
   Noscamus atque Filium,
   Teque utriusque Spiritum
   Credamus omni tempore.

7 Deo Patri sit gloria,
   Et Filio, qui a mortuis
   Surrexit, ac Paraclito
   In saeculorum saecula.

Veni Sancte Spiritus.

HOLY Spirit! Lord of light!
From thy clear celestial height,
   Thy pure beaming radiance give:

Come, Thou Father of the poor!
Come, with treasures which endure!
   Come, Thou Light of all that live!

Thou of all consolers best,
Visiting the troubled breast,
   Dost refreshing peace bestow;

Thou in toil art comfort sweet;
Pleasant coolness in the heat;
   Solace in the midst of woe.

Light immortal! light divine!
Visit Thou these hearts of thine,
   And our inmost being fill:

If Thou take thy grace away,
Nothing pure in man will stay;
   All his good is turn'd to ill.

Heal our wounds — our strength renew;
On our dryness pour thy dew;
   Wash the stains of guilt away:

Bend the stubborn heart and will;
Melt the frozen, warm the chill;
   Guide the steps that go astray.

Thou, on those who evermore
Thee confess and Thee adore,
   In thy sevenfold gifts, descend:

Give them comfort when they die;
Give them life with Thee on high;
   Give them joys which never end.

TRINITY-SUNDAY.
MORNING.

Summae Parens clementiae.

O THOU eternal Source of Love!
   Ruler of nature's scheme!
In Substance One, in Persons Three!
   Omniscient and Supreme!

Be nigh to us when we arise;
   And, at the break of day,
With wakening body wake the soul,
   Her meed of praise to pay.

To God the Father, glory be,
    And to his only Son;
The same, O Holy Ghost! to Thee,
    While ceaseless ages run.

EVENING.

Jam sol recedit igneus.

Now doth the fiery sun decline: —
Thou, Unity eternal! shine;
Thou, Trinity, thy blessings pour,
And make our hearts with love run o'er.

Thee in the hymns of morn we praise;
To Thee our voice at eve we raise;
Oh, grant us, with thy Saints on high,
Thee through all time to glorify.

Praise to the Father, with the Son,
And Holy Spirit, Three in One;
As ever was in ages past,
And shall be so while ages last.

CORPUS CHRISTI.

Sacris solemniis juncta sint gaudia.

    LET us with hearts renew'd,
      Our grateful homage pay;
And welcome with triumphant songs
    This ever-blessed day.

    Upon this hallow'd night
    Christ with his brethren ate,

Obedient to the olden law,
    The Paseh before Him set.

Which done,—Himself entire,
    The true Incarnate God,
Alike on each, alike on all,
    His sacred hands bestow'd.

He gave his Flesh; He gave
    His precious Blood; and said,
"Receive, and drink ye all of this,
    For your salvation shed."

Thus did the Lord appoint
    This Sacrifice sublime,
And made his Priests its ministers
    Through all the bounds of time.

Farewell to types! Henceforth
    We feed on Angels' food
The guilty slave — oh, wonder! — eats
    The Body of his God!

O Blessed Three in One!
    Visit our hearts, we pray;
And lead us on through thine own paths
    To thy eternal Day.

Lauda Sion Salvatorem.

1 SION, lift thy voice, and Sing;
    Praise thy Saviour and thy King;
        Praise with hymns thy Shepherd true;
    Strive thy best to praise Him well;
    Yet doth He all praise excel;
        None can ever reach his due.

2 See to-day before us laid
   The living and life-giving Bread!
      Theme for praise and joy profound!
   The same which at the sacred board
   Was, by our Incarnate Lord,
      Given to his Apostles round.

3 Let the praise be loud and high;
   Sweet and tranquil be the joy
      Felt to-day in every breast;
   On this Festival divine,
   Which records the origin
      Of the glorious Eucharist.

4 On this Table of the King,
   Our new Paschal offering
      Brings to end the olden rite;
   Here, for empty shadows fled,
   Is Reality instead;
      Here, instead of darkness, Light.

5 His own act, at supper seated,
   Christ ordain'd to be repeated,
      In his Memory divine;
   Wherefore now, with adoration,
   We the Host of our salvation
      Consecrate from bread and wine.

6 Hear what holy Church maintaineth,
   That the bread its substance changeth
      Into Flesh, the wine to Blood.
   Doth it pass thy comprehending?
   Faith, the law of sight transcending,
      Leaps to things not understood.

7 Here, beneath these signs, are hidden
    Priceless things, to sense forbidden;
        Signs, not things, are all we see:
    Flesh from bread, and Blood from wine;
    Yet is Christ, in either sign,
        All entire, confess'd to be.

8 They too, who of Him partake,
    Sever not, nor rend, nor break,
        But entire their Lord receive.
    Whether one or thousands eat,
    All receive the self-same meat,
        Nor the less for others leave.

9 Both the wicked and the good
    Eat of this celestial Food;
        But with ends how opposite!
    Here 'tis life; and there 'tis death;
    The same, yet issuing to each
        In a difference infinite.

10 Nor a single doubt retain,
    When they break the Host in twain,
    But that in each part remains
        What was in the whole before;
    Since the simple sign alone
    Suffers change in state or form,
    The Signified remaining One
        And the Same for evermore.

    [Ecce panis angelorum.]

11 Lo! upon the Altar lies,
    Hidden deep from human eyes,
    Bread of Angels from the skies,
        Made the food of mortal man
    Children's meat to dogs denied;

In old types foresignified;
In the manna Heav'n—supplied,
    Isaac, and the Paschal Lamb.

12 Jesu! Shepherd of the sheep!
Thou thy flock in safety keep.
Living Bread! thy life supply;
Strengthen us, or else we die;
    Fill us with celestial grace:
Thou, who feedest us below!
Source of all we have or know!
Grant that with thy Saints above,
Sitting at the feast of love,
    We may see Thee face to face.

  1 LAUDA, Sion, Salvatorem,
    Lauda Ducem et Pastorem,
    In hymnis et canticis.
    Quantum potes, tantum aude;
    Quia major omni laude,
    Nec laudare sufficis.

  2 Laudis thema specialis,
    Panis vivus et vitalis,
    Hodie proponitur.
    Quem in sacrae mensa coenae,
    Turbae fratrum duodenae
    Datum non ambigitur.

  3 Sit laus plena, sit sonora,
    Sit jucunda, sit decora,
    Mentis jubilatio.
    Dies enim solemnis agitur,
    In qua mensae prima recolitur
    Hujus institutio.

4 In hac mensa novi Regis,
   Novum pascha novae legis,
   Phase vetus terminat.
   Vetustatem novitas,
   Umbram fugat veritas,
   Noctem lux eliminat.

5 Quod in coena Christus gessit,
   Faciendum hoc expressit
   In sui memoriam.
   Docti sacris institutis,
   Panem, vinum, in salutis
   Consecramus hostiam.

6 Dogma datur Christianis,
   Quod in carnem transit panis,
   Et Vinum in sanguinem.
   Quod non capis, quod non vides,
   Animosa firmat fides,
   Praeter rerum ordinem.

7 Sub diversis speciebus
   Signis tantum et non rebus,
   Latent res eximiae.
   Caro cibus, sanguis potus:
   Manet tamen Christus totus
   Sub utraque specie.

8 A sumente non concisus,
   Non confractus, non divisus.
   Integer accipitur.
   Sumit unus, sumunt mille,
   Quantum isti, tantum ille,
   Nec sumptus consumitur.

9 Sumunt boni, sumunt mali:
   Sorte tamen inaequali,
   Vitae vel interitus.
   Mors est malis, vita bonis,
   Vide paris sumptionis,
   Quam sit dispar exitus.

10 Fracto demum sacramento,
   Ne vacilles, sed memento,
   Tantum esse sub fragmento,
   Quantum toto tegitur.
   Nulla rei fit scissura:
   Signi tantum fit fractura:
   Qua, nec status nec statura
   Signati minuitur.

11 Ecce panis angelorum,
   Factus cibus viatorum:
   Vere panis filiorum,
   Non mittendus canibus;
   In figuris praesignatur,
   Cum Isaac immolatur:
   Agnus paschae deputatur:
   Datur manna patribus.

12 Bone Pastor, panis vere,
   Jesu nostri miserere:
   Tu nos pasce, nos tuere:
   Tu nos bona fac videre
   In terra viventium.
   Tu qui cuncta scis et vales,
   Qui nos pascis hic mortales:
   Tuos ibi commensales,
   Cohaeredes et sodales
   Fac sanctorum civium.

FEAST OF THE MOST SACRED HEART OF JESUS.
FRIDAY AFTER THE OCTAVE OF CORPUS CHRISTI.

Summi Parentis filio.

> To Christ, the Prince of Peace,
> And Son of God most high,
> The Father of the world to come, —
> Sing we with holy joy.

> Deep in his heart for us
> The wound of love He bore; —
> That love, which still He kindles in
> The hearts that Him adore.

> O Jesu! Victim blest!
> What else but love divine
> Could Thee constrain to open thus
> That sacred Heart of thine?

> O Fount of endless life!
> O Spring of waters clear!
> O Flame celestial, cleansing all
> Who unto Thee draw near!

> Hide me in thy dear Heart,
> For thither do I fly;
> There seek thy grace through life, in death
> Thine immortality.

> Praise to the Father be;
> Praise to his only Son;
> Praise to the blessed Paraclete,
> While endless ages run.

Quicunque certum quaeritis.

ALL ye who seek a certain cure
    In trouble and distress,
Whatever sorrow vex the mind,
    Or guilt the soul oppress:

Jesus, who gave Himself for you
    Upon the Cross to die,
Opens to you his sacred Heart, —
    Oh, to that Heart draw nigh!

Ye hear how kindly He invites;
    Ye hear his words so blest;—
"All ye that labor, come to Me,
    And I will give you rest."

What meeker than the Saviour's Heart?
    As on the Cross He lay,
It did his murderers forgive,
    And for their pardon pray.

O Heart! thou joy of Saints on high!
    Thou Hope of sinners here!
Attracted by those loving words,
    To Thee I lift my prayer.

Wash Thou my wounds in that dear Blood
    Which forth from Thee doth flow;
New grace, new hope inspire;
    A new and better heart bestow.

PURIFICATION OF THE B. VIRGIN MARY.

February 2.

Templi sacratas pande Sion fores.

O SION! open wide thy gates;
    Let figures disappear;
A Priest and Victim both in one,
    The Truth Himself is here.

No more the simple flock shall bleed. —
    Behold the Father's Son!
Himself to his own Altar comes
    For sinners to atone.

Conscious of hidden Deity,
    The lowly Virgin brings
Her new-born Babe, with two young doves,
    Her tender offerings.

The hoary Simeon sees at last
    His Lord so long desired,
And hails, with Anna, Israel's hope,
    With sudden rapture fired.

But silent knelt the Mother blest
    Of the yet silent Word;
And pondering all things in her heart,
    With speechless praise adored.

Praise to the Father and the Son;
    Praise to the Spirit be;
Praise to the blessed Three in One,
    Through all eternity.

FEAST OF ST. JOSEPH.

March 19.

Caelitum Joseph decus atque nostrae.

JOSEPH our certain hope of life!
    Glory of earth and Heaven!
Thou Pillar of the world! to thee
    Be praise eternal given.

Thee, as Salvation's minister,
    The mighty Maker chose;
As Foster-father of the Word;
    As Mary's spotless Spouse.

With joy thou sawest Him new born,
    Of whom the Prophets sang:
Him in a manger didst adore,
    From whom Creation sprang.

The Lord of lords, and King of kings,
    Ruler of sky and sea,
Whom Heaven, and Earth, and Hell obey,
    Was subject unto thee.

Blest Trinity! vouchsafe to us,
    Through Joseph's merits high,
To mount the Heavenly seats, and reign
    With him eternally.

Quicungue sanus vivere.

To all who would holily live,
    To all who would happily die,

St. Joseph is ready to give
    Sure guidance, and help from on high.

Of Mary the Spouse undefiled,
    Just, holy, and pure of all stain,
He asks of his own Foster-Child;
    And needs but to ask to obtain.

[Here the first stanza is repeated.]

To all who would holily live,
    To all who would happily die,
St. Joseph is ready to give
    Sure guidance, and help from on high.

In the manger that Child he adored,
    And nursed Him in exile and flight;
Him, lost in his boyhood, deplored;
    And found with amaze and delight.
        To all, &c., *as above.*

The Maker of Heaven and Earth
    By the labor of Joseph was fed;
The Son by an infinite birth
    Submissive to Joseph was made.
        To all, &c.

And when his last hour drew nigh,
    Oh, full of all joy was his breast;
Seeing Jesus and Mary close by,
    As he tranquilly slumber'd to rest.
        To all, &c.

All praise to the Father above;
    All praise to his glorious Son
All praise to the Spirit of love;

While the days of eternity run.
To all, &c.

HYMN TO ST. JOSEPH.

HAIL! holy Joseph, hail!
Husband of Mary, hail!
Chaste as the lily flower
In Eden's peaceful vale.

Hail! holy Joseph, hail!
Father of Christ esteemed!
Father be thou to those
Thy Foster-Son redeem'd.

Hail! holy Joseph, hail!
Prince of the House of God,
May his best graces be
By thy Sweet hands bestow'd.

Hail! holy Joseph, hail!
Comrade of angels, hail!
Cheer then the hearts that faint,
And guide the steps that fail.

Hail! holy Joseph, hail!
God's choice wert thou alone;
To thee the Word made flesh
Was subject as a Son.

Hail! holy Joseph, hail!
Teach us our flesh to tame,
And, Mary, keep the hearts
That love thy husband's name.

Mother of Jesus! bless,
And bless, ye Saints on high,
All meek and simple souls
That to Saint Joseph cry.
     Amen.

THE PATRONAGE OF ST. JOSEPH.
THIRD SUNDAY AFTER EASTER.

DEAR Husband of Mary! dear Nurse of her Child!
Life's ways are full weary, the desert is wild;
Bleak sands are all round us, no home can we see;
Sweet Spouse of our Lady! we lean upon thee.

For thou to the pilgrim art Father and Guide,
And Jesus and Mary felt safe by thy side;
Ah! blessed Saint Joseph! how safe should I be,
Sweet Spouse of our Lady! if thou wert with me!

O blessed Saint Joseph! how great was thy worth,
The one chosen shadow of God upon earth,
The Father of Jesus — ah! then wilt thou be,
Sweet Spouse of our Lady! a father to me?

Thou hast not forgotten the long dreary road,
When Mary took turns with thee, bearing thy God;
Yet light was that burden, none lighter could be:
Sweet Spouse of our Lady! O canst thou bear me?

A cold, thankless heart, and a mean love of ease,
What weights, blessed Patron! more galling than these?
My life, my past life, thy clear vision may see:
Sweet Spouse of our Lady! O canst thou love me?

Ah! give me thy Burden to bear for a while;
Let me kiss his warm lips, and adore his sweet smile;

With her Babe in my arms, surely Mary will be,
Sweet Spouse of our Lady! my pleader with thee!

When the treasures of God were unshelter'd on earth,
Safe keeping was found for them both in thy worth;
O Father of Jesus! be father to me,
Sweet Spouse of our Lady! and I will love thee.

God chose thee for Jesus and Mary — wilt thou
Forgive a poor exile for choosing thee now?
There is no Saint in Heaven I worship like thee,
Sweet Spouse of our Lady! O deign to love me!

ANNUNCIATION OF THE BLESSED VIRGIN MARY.

March 25.

Quis te canat mortalium?

WHAT mortal tongue can sing thy praise,
    Dear Mother of the Lord? —
To angels only it belongs
    Thy glory to record.

Who born of man can penetrate
    Thy soul's majestic shrine?
Who can thy mighty gifts unfold,
    Or rightly them divine?

Say, Virgin, what sweet force was that
    Which from the Father's breast,
Drew forth his coeternal Son,
    To be thy bosom's guest?

'Twas not thy guileless faith alone,
    That lifted thee so high;

'Twas not thy pure seraphic love,
    Or peerless chastity:

But, oh! it was thy lowliness,
    Well pleasing to the Lord,
That made Thee worthy to become
    The Mother of the Word.

Oh, Loftiest! whose humility
    So sweet it was to see!
That God, forgetful of Himself,
    Abased Himself to Thee!

Praise to the Father, with the Son,
    And Holy Ghost, through Whom
The Word eternal was conceived
    Within the Virgin's womb.

FEAST OF ST. MICHAEL.

May 8.

Te Splendor et virtus Patris.

O JESU! life-spring of the soul!
    The Father's Power, and Glory bright!
Thee with the Angels we extol;
    From Thee they draw their life and light.

Thy thousand thousand hosts are spread,
    Embattled o'er the azure sky;
But Michael bears thy standard dread,
    And lifts the mighty Cross on high.

He in that Sign the rebel powers
    Did with their Dragon Prince expel;

And hurl'd them from the Heaven's high towers,
    Down like a thunderbolt to hell.

Grant us with Michael still, O Lord,
    Against the Prince of Pride to fight;
So may a crown be our reward,
    Before the Lamb's pure throne of light.

Now to the Father, and the Son
    Who rose from death, all glory be;
With Thee, O holy Comforter!
    Henceforth through all eternity.

[Within the Octave of the Ascension.]

Glory to Jesus, who returns
    In pomp triumphant to the sky,
With Thee, O Father, and with Thee,
    O Holy Ghost, eternally.

THE BLESSED VLRGIN MARY THE HELP OF CHRISTIANS.

May 24.

Te Redemptoris Dominique nostri.

MOTHER of our Lord and Saviour!
    First in beauty as in power!
Glory of the Christian nations!
    Ready help in trouble's hour!

Though the gates of Hell against us
    With profoundest fury rage;
Though the ancient Foe assault us,
    And his fiercest battle wage;

Naught can hurt the pure in spirit,
    Who upon thine aid rely;

At thy hand secure of gaining
    Strength and mercy from on high.

Safe beneath thy mighty shelter, —
    Though a thousand hosts combine,
All must fall or flee before us,
    Scatter'd by an arm divine.

Firm as once on holy Sion,
    David's tower rear'd its height;
With a glorious rampart girded,
    And with glistening armor bright:

So th' Almighty's Virgin Mother
    Stands in strength for evermore;
From Satanic hosts defending
    All who her defence implore.

Through the everlasting ages,
    Blessed Trinity, to Thee!
Father, Son, and Holy Spirit,
    Praise and endless glory be.

SS. PETER AND PAUL, APOSTLES.

June 29.

Decora lux aeternitatis auream.

BATHED in eternity's all-beauteous beam,
And opening into Heaven a path sublime,
Welcome the golden day! which heralds in
The Apostolic Chiefs, whose glory fills all time!

Peter and Paul, the Fathers of great Rome!
Now sitting in the Senate of the skies!

One by the Cross, the other by the Sword,
Sent to their thrones on high, and life's eternal prize.

O happy Rome! whom that most glorious blood
Forever consecrates while ages flow;
Thou, thus empurpled, art more beautiful
Than all that doth appear most beautiful below.

Praise, blessing, majesty, through endless days,
Be to the Trinity immortal given;
Who, in pure Unity, profoundly sways
Eternally all things alike in earth and Heaven.

FEAST OF ST. JOHN THE BAPTIST.

June 24.

O nimis felix meritique celsi.

O BLESSED Saint, of snow-white purity!
    Dweller in wastes forlorn!
O mightiest of the Martyr host on high!
    Greatest of Prophets born!

Of all the diadems that on the brows
    Of Saints in glory shine,
Not one with brighter, purer halo glows,
    In Heaven's high Court, than thine.

Oh! upon us thy tender, pitying gaze
    Cast down from thy dread throne;
Straighten our crooked, smooth our rugged ways,
    And break our hearts of stone.

So may the world's Redeemer find us meet
    To offer Him a place,

Where He may set his ever-blessed feet,
    Coming with gifts of grace.

Praise in the Heavens to Thee, O First and
    The Trine eternal God!
Spare, Jesu, spare thy people, whom Thou hast last,
    Redeem'd with thine own blood.

VISITATION OF THE BLESSED VIRGIN MARY.

July 2.

Quo sanctus ardor te rapit.

WHITHER thus, in holy rapture,
    Princely Maiden, art Thou bent?
Why so fleetly art Thou speeding
    Up the mountain's rough ascent?

Fill'd with the eternal Godhead!
    Glowing with the Spirit's flame!
Love it is that bears Thee onward,
    And supports thy tender frame.

Lo! thine aged cousin claims Thee,
    Claims thy sympathy and care;
God her shame from her hath taken;
    He hath heard her fervent prayer.

Blessed Mothers! joyful meeting!
    Thou in her, the hand of God,
She in Thee, with lips inspired,
    Owns the Mother of her Lord.

As the sun his face concealing,
    In a cloud withdraws from sight,

So in Mary then lay hidden
  He who is the world's true light.

Honor, glory, virtue, merit,
  Be to Thee, O Virgin's Son!
With the Father, and the Spirit,
  While eternal ages run.

FEAST OF ST. ANNE, MOTHER OF THE BLESSED VIRGIN MARY.

July 26.

Clarae diei gaudiis.

SPOTLESS Anna! Juda's glory!
  Through the Church from East to West,
Every tongue proclaims thy praises,
  Holy Mary's Mother blest!

Saintly Kings and priestly Sires
  Blended in thy sacred line;
Thou in virtue, all before thee
  Didst excel by grace divine.

Link'd in bonds of purest wedlock,
  Thine it was for us to bear,
By the favor of High Heaven,
  Our eternal Virgin Star.

From thy stem in beauty budded
  Ancient Jesse's mystic rod;
Earth from thee received the Mother
  Of th' Almighty Son of God.

All the human race benighted
    In the depths of darkness lay;
When in Anne, it saw the dawning
    Of the long-expected day.

Honor, glory, virtue, merit,
    Be to Thee, O Virgin's Son,
With the Father and the Spirit,
    While eternal ages run.

FEAST OF THE TRANSFIGURATION.

August 6.

Quicunque Christum quaeritis.

ALL ye who seek, in hope and love,
For your dear Lord, look up above!
Where, traced upon the azure sky,
Faith may a glorious form descry.

Lo! on the trembling verge of light
A something all divinely bright!
Immortal, infinite, sublime!
Older than chaos, space, or time!

Hail, Thou, the Gentiles' mighty Lord!
All hail, O Israel's King adored!
To Abraham sworn in ages past,
And to his seed while earth shall last.

To Thee the prophets witness bear;
Of Thee the Father doth declare,
That all who would his glory see,
Must hear and must believe in Thee.

To Jesus, from the proud conceal'd,
But evermore to babes reveal'd,
All glory with the Father be,
And Holy Ghost, eternally.

ASSUMPTION OF THE BLESSED VIRGIN MARY.

August 15.

O vos aetherei plaudite cives.

REJOICE, O ye Spirits and Angels on high!
    This day the pure Mother of Love
By death was set free; and ascending the sky,
Was welcomed by Jesus, with triumph and joy,
    To the Courts of his glory above!

O Virgin divine! what treasures are thine!
    What power and splendor untold!
With flesh thou hadst clothed the Lord of all might; —
He clothes Thee in turn with his infinite light,
    And a radiant vesture of gold.

He, who on thy breast found nurture and rest,
    Is now thy ineffable Food;
And He, who from Thee in the flesh lay conceal'd,
Now gives Thee, beholding his glory reveal'd,
    To drink from the fulness of God.

Through thy Virginal womb what graces have come!
    What glories encompass thy throne!
Where next to thy Son, thou sittest a Queen,
Exalted on high, above Angels and men!
    Inferior to Godhead alone!

Then hear us, we pray, on this blessed day;
    Remember we also are thine;
And deign for thy children with Jesus to plead,
That He may forgive us, and grant us in need
    His strength and protection divine.

All praise to the Father, who chose for his Son
    A Mother, the daughter of Eve;
All praise to the glorious Child of her womb;
All praise to the infinite Spirit, by Whom
    Her glory it was to conceive.

ST. ROSE OF LIMA.

August 30.

FIRST flow'ret of the desert wild!
    Whose leaves the sweets of grace exhale,
We greet thee, Lima's sainted child —
    Rose of America — all hail!

When first appear'd the infant smile,
    Beaming upon thy features meek,
It seem'd as if there blush'd, the while,
    The Rose-bud on thy virgin cheek.

And hence thy name, St. Rose, was given,
    Not by thy earthly parents' choice,
But by the holy Queen of Heaven,
    Who bade thee in that name rejoice.

Transplanted from the worldly gaze,
    Which sometimes taints the fairest flowers,
In solitude thou lov'dst to praise
    Thy spouse amid Religion's bowers.

There oft thy mind, too pure, too high,
    For this low world of sin and strife,
Held blest communion with the sky,
    Enjoying Heaven in mortal life.

And once, amid thy rapturous prayer,
    Thy heavenly Spouse himself came down,
Most sweetly breathing in thine ear,
    "Rose of my heart, receive thy crown."

And whilst amid his glories now,
    Thou seest him face to face — oh deign,
St. Rose, to hear thy suppliants' vow,
    That grace and glory we may gain.

FEAST OF THE NATIVITY OF THE BLESSED VIRGIN MARY.

September 8.

Aurora quae Solem paris.

SWEET Morn! thou Parent of the Sun!
    And Daughter of the same!
What joy and gladness, through thy birth,
    This day to mortals came!

Clothed in the Sun I see Thee stand,
    The Moon beneath thy feet,
The Stars above thy sacred head
    A radiant coronet.

Thrones and Dominions gird Thee round,
    The Armies of the sky;
Pure streams of glory from Thee flow,
    All bathed in Deity!

Terrific as the banner'd line
   Of battle's dread array!
Before Thee tremble Hell and Death,
   And own thy mighty sway:

While crush'd beneath thy dauntless foot,
   The Serpent writhes in vain,
Smit by a deadly stroke, and bound
   In an eternal chain.

O Mightiest! pray for us, that He
   Who came through Thee of yore,
May come to dwell within our hearts,
   And never quit us more.

Praise to the Father, with the Son,
   And Holy Ghost, through Whom
The Word eternal was conceived
   Within the Virgin's womb.

EXALTATION OF THE HOLY CROSS.

September 14.

Pange lingua gloriosi.[2]

SING, my tongue, the Saviour's glory;
   Tell his triumph far and wide;
Tell aloud the famous story
   Of his Body crucified;
How upon the Cross a Victim,
   Vanquishing in death, He died.

---

[2] The same for the Feast of the FINDING OF THE HOLY CROSS, May 3.

Eating of the Tree forbidden,
    Man had sunk in Satan's snare,
When our pitying Creator
    Did this second Tree prepare;
Destined, many ages later,
    That first evil to repair.

Such the order God appointed
    When for sin He would atone;
To the Serpent thus opposing
    Schemes yet deeper than his own;
Thence the remedy procuring,
    Whence the fatal wound had come.

So when new at length the fulness
    Of the sacred time drew nigh,
Then the Son, the world's Creator,
    Left his Father's throne on high;
From a Virgin's womb appearing,
    Clothed in our mortality.

All within a lowly manger,
    Lo, a tender Babe He lies!
See his gentle Virgin mother
    Lull to sleep his infant cries!
While the limbs of God Incarnate
    Round with swathing bands she ties.

Blessing, honor everlasting,
    To the immortal Deity;
To the Father, Son, and Spirit,
    Equal praises ever be;
Glory through the earth and Heaven
    To Trinity in Unity.

    [The same continued.]

Lustra sex qui jam peregit.

THUS did Christ to perfect manhood
    In our mortal flesh attain;
Then of his free choice He goeth
    To a death of bitter pain;
And as a lamb, upon the altar
    Of the Cross, for us is slain.

Lo, with gall his thirst He quenches!
    See the thorns upon his brow!
Nails his tender flesh are rending!
    See, his side is open'd now!
Whence, to cleanse the whole creation,
    Streams of blood and water flow.

Lofty Tree, bend down thy branches,
    To embrace thy sacred load;
Oh, relax the native tension
    Of that all too rigid wood;
Gently, gently bear the members
    Of thy dying King and God.

Tree, which solely wast found worthy
    The world's great Victim to sustain;
Harbor from the raging tempest!
    Ark, that saved the world again!
Tree, with sacred Blood anointed
    Of the Lamb for sinners slain.

Blessing, honor everlasting,
    To the immortal Deity;
To the Father, Son, and Spirit,
    Equal praises ever be:
Glory through the earth and Heaven
    To Trinity in Unity.

SEVEN DOLORS OF THE BLESSED VIRGIN MARY.
SUNDAY AFTER THE OCTAVE OF THE NATIVITY.

O quot undis lachrymarum.

WHAT a sea of tears and sorrow
 Did the soul of Mary toss
To and fro upon its billows,
 While she wept her bitter loss;
In her arms her Jesus holding,
 Torn but newly from the Cross!

O that mournful Virgin Mother!
 See her tears how fast they flow
Down upon his mangled body,
 Wounded side, and thorny brow;
While his hands and feet she kisses, —
 Picture of immortal woe!

Oft and oft his arms and bosom
 Fondly straining to her own;
Oft her pallid lips imprinting
 On each wound of her dear Son;
Till at last, in swoons of anguish,
 Sense and consciousness are gone.

Gentle Mother, we beseech thee,
 By thy tears and trouble sore;
By the death of thy dear Offspring;
 By the bloody wounds He bore;
Touch our hearts with that true sorrow
 Which afflicted thee of yore.

To the Father everlasting,
 And the Son, who reigns on high,
With the coeternal Spirit,

Trinity in Unity,
Be salvation, honor, blessing,
Now and through eternity.

FEAST OF THE MOST HOLY GUARDIAN ANGELS.

October 2.

AEterne Rector siderum.

RULER of the dread immense!
    Maker of this mighty frame!
Whose eternal Providence
    Governs and upholds the same!

Low before thy face we bend;
    Hear our supplicating cries;
And thy light eternal send,
    With the freshly dawning skies.

King of kings! and Lord most high!
    This of thy dear love we pray, —
May thy Guardian Angel nigh
    Keep us from all sin this day.

May he crush the deadly wiles
    Of the envious Serpent's art,
Ever spreading cunning toils
    Round about the thoughtless heart.

May he scatter ruthless war,
    Ere to this our shore it come;
Plague and famine drive afar;
    Fix securely peace at home.

Father, Son, and Holy Ghost,
    Everlasting Trinity!
Guard, by thy Angelic host,
    Us, who put our trust in Thee.

MATERNITY OF THE BLESSED VIRGIN MARY.

Second Sunday in October.

Te Mater alma Numinis.

MOTHER of Almighty God!
    Suppliant at thy feet we pray;
Shelter us from Satan's fraud,
    Safe beneath thy wing this day.

'Twas by reason of our Fall,
    In our first Forefather's crime,
That the mighty Lord of all
    Raised thee to thy rank sublime.

Oh! then upon Adam's race
    Look thou with a pitying eye;
And entreat of Jesus grace,
    Till He lay his anger by.

Honor, glory, virtue, merit,
    Be to Thee, O Virgin's Son,
With the Father and the Spirit,
    While eternal ages run.

PURITY OF THE BLESSED VIRGIN MARY.

Third Sunday in October.

O stella Jacob fulgida.

STAR of Jacob, ever beaming
    With a radiance all divine!
'Mid the stars of highest Heaven
    Glows no purer ray than thine.

All in stoles of snowy brightness,
    Unto thee the Angels sing;
Unto thee the virgin choirs, —
    Mother of th' eternal King!

Joyful in thy path they scatter
    Roses white and lilies fair;
Yet with thy chaste bosom's whiteness,
    Rose nor lily may compare.

Oh! that this low earth of ours,
    Answering th' angelic strain,
With thy praises might re-echo,
    Till the Heavens replied again.

Honor, glory, virtue, merit,
    Be to Thee, O Virgin's Son!
With the Father, and the Spirit,
    While eternal ages run.

ALL SAINTS' DAY.

November 1.

Salutis aeternae dator.

GIVER of life, eternal Lord!
    Thy own redeem'd defend;
Mother of Grace! thy children save,
    And help them to the end.

Ye thousand thousand Angel Hosts!
    Assist us in our need;
Ye Patriarchs! with the Prophet Choir!
    For our forgiveness plead.

Herald of Christ! and Thou who still
    Dost Heaven's dread keys retain!
Ye glorious Apostles all!
    Unloose our guilty chain.

Army of Martyrs! holy Priests!
    In beauteous array!
Ye happy troops of Virgins chaste!
    Wash all our sins away.

All ye who high above the stars
    In heavenly glory reign!
May we, through your blest prayers, the gifts
    Of endless life obtain.

Praise, honor, to the Father be,
    Praise to his only Son;
Praise to the Spirit Paraclete,
    While ceaseless ages run.

IMMACULATE CONCEPTION OF THE BLESSED VIRGIN MARY.[3]

December 8.
[Hymns from the Office.]

AT MATINS.

Salve mundi domina.

HAIL, Queen of the Heavens!
Hail, Mistress of earth!
Hail, Virgin most pure,
Of immaculate birth!
Clear Star of the Morning,
In beauty enshrined!
O Lady, make speed
To the help of mankind!

Thee God in the depth
Of eternity chose;
And form'd thee all fair,
As his glorious Spouse;
And call'd thee his Word's
Own Mother to be,
By whom He created
The earth, sky, and sea.

---

[3] The Blessed Virgin Mary, "CONCEIVED WITHOUT SIN," is the Patroness of the United States. The Feast is *solemnized* on the Sunday within the Octave.

AT PRIME.

Salve Virgo sapiens.

HAIL, Virgin most wise!
Hail, Deity's Shrine,
With seven fair pillars
And Table divine!
Preserved from the guilt
Which has come on us all!
Exempt in the womb
From the taint of the Fall!

O new Star of Jacob!
Of Angels the Queen!
O Gate of the Saints!
O Mother of men!
O terrible as
The embattled array!
Be thou of the Faithful
The refuge and stay.

AT TERCE.

Salve arca foederis.

HAIL, Solomon's Throne!
Pure Ark of the Law!
Fair Rainbow and Bush
Which the Patriarch saw!
Hail, Gedeon's Fleece
Hail, blossoming Rod!
Samson's sweet Honeycomb!
Portal of God!

Well fitting it was
That a Son so divine
Should preserve from all touch
Of Original Sin;
Nor suffer by smallest
Defect to be stain'd
That Mother, whom He
For Himself had ordain'd.

AT SEXT.

Salve Virgo puerpera.

HAIL, Virginal Mother!
Hail, Purity's Cell!
Fair Shrine where the Trinity
Loveth to dwell!
Hail, Garden of pleasure!
Celestial Balm!
Cedar of Chastity!
Martyrdom's Palm!

Thou Land set apart
From uses profane,
And free from the curse
Which in Adam began!
Thou City of God!
Thou Gate of the East!
In thee is all grace,
O Joy of the Blest!

AT NONE.

Salve urbs refugii

HAIL, City of refuge!
Hail, David's high tower!
With battlements crown'd,
And girded with power!
Fill'd at thy Conception
With Love and with Light!
The Dragon by Thee
Was shorn of his might.

O Woman most valiant!
O Judith thrice blest!
As David was nursed
In fair Abishag's breast;
As the saviour of Egypt
Upon Rachel's knee;
So the world's great Redeemer
Was fondled by Thee.

AT VESPERS.

Salve horologium.

HAIL, Dial of Achaz!
On Thee the true Sun
Told backward the course
Which from old He had run;
And, that man might be raised,
Submitting to shame,
A little more low
Than the Angels became.

Thou, wrapt in the blaze
Of His infinite Light,
Dost shine as the morn
On the confines of night;
As the Moon on the lost
Through Obscurity dawns;
The Serpent's Destroyer!
A Lily 'mid thorns!

AT COMPLINE.

Salve Virgo florens.

HAIL, Mother most pure!
Hail, Virgin renown'd!
Hail, Queen with the stars
As a diadem crown'd!
Above all the Angels
In glory untold,
Standing next to the King,
In a vesture of gold!

O Mother of mercy!
O Star of the wave!
O Hope of the guilty!
O Light of the grave!
Through Thee may we come
To the Haven of rest;
And see Heaven's King
In the courts of the Blest.

THE COMMENDATION.

Supplices offerimus.

THESE praises and prayers
I lay at thy feet,
O Virgin of Virgins!
O Mary most Sweet!
Be Thou my true guide
Through this pilgrimage here,
And stand by my side
When death draweth near.

THE IMMACULATE CONCEPTION.

Sine labe concepta.

O PUREST of creatures! sweet Mother! sweet Maid!
The one spotless womb wherein Jesus was laid!
Dark night hath come down on us, Mother! and we
Look out for thy shining, sweet Star of the Sea!

Deep night hath come down on this rough-spoken world,
And the banners of darkness are boldly unfurl'd;
And the tempest-tost Church — all her eyes are on thee,
They look to thy Shining, Sweet Star of the Sea!

The Church doth what God had first taught her to do;
He look'd o'er the world to find hearts that were true;
Through the ages He look'd, and He found none but thee,
And He loved thy clear shining, sweet Star of the Sea!

He gazed on thy soul; it was spotless and fair
For the empire of sin — it had never been there;
None had e'er own'd thee, dear Mother! but He,
And He bless'd thy clear shining, sweet Star of the Sea!

Earth gave Him one lodging; 'twas deep in thy breast,
And God found a home where the sinner finds rest;
His home and his hiding-place, both were in thee,
He was won by thy Shining, sweet Star of the Sea!

O blissful and calm was the wonderful rest
That thou gavest thy God in thy virginal breast;
For the Heaven He left He found Heaven in thee,
And He shone in thy shining, sweet Star of the Sea!

To sinners what comfort, to angels what mirth,
That God found one creature unfallen on earth,
One spot where his Spirit untroubled could be,
The depths of thy Shining, sweet Star of the Sea!

So age after age in the Church hath gone round,
And the Saints new inventions of homage have found,
New titles of honor, new honors for thee,
New love for thy shining, sweet Star of the Sea!

And now from the Church of all lands thy dear name
Comes borne on the breath of one mighty acclaim;
Men call on their Father, that He should decree
A new gem to thy shining, sweet Star of the Sea!

O shine on us brighter than ever, then, shine!
For the primest of honors, dear Mother! is thine;
"Conceived without sin," thy new title shall be,
Clear light from thy birth-spring, sweet Star of the Sea!

So worship we God in these rude latter days;
So worship we Jesus our Love, when we praise
His wonderful grace in the gifts He gave thee,
The gift of clear shining, sweet Star of the Sea!

Deep night hath come down on us, Mother! deep night,
And we need more than ever the guide of thy light;

For the darker the night is, the brighter should be
Thy beautiful shining, sweet Star of the Sea!

EVENING HYMN TO THE BLESSED VIRGIN MARY.

Ave maris Stella.

1. GENTLE Star of ocean!
    Portal of the sky!
   Ever Virgin Mother
    Of the Lord most High!

2. Oh! by Gabriel's Ave,
    Utter'd long ago,
   Eva's name reversing,
    Stablish peace below.

3. Break the captive's fetters;
    Light on blindness pour;
   All our ills expelling,
    Every bliss implore.

4. Show thyself a Mother;
    Offer Him our sighs,
   Who for us Incarnate
    Did not thee despise.

5. Virgin of all Virgins!
    To thy shelter take us:
   Gentlest of the gentle!
    Chaste and gentle make us.

6. Still as on we journey,
    Help our weak endeavor;
   Till with thee and Jesus
    We rejoice forever.

7 Through the highest Heaven,
    To the Almighty Three,
Father, Son, and Spirit,
    One same glory be.

1 AVE maris stella,
Dei mater alma,
Atque semper virgo,
Felix coeli porta.

2 Sumens illud Ave
Gabrielis ore,
Funda nos in pace,
Mutans Evae nomen.

3 Solve vincla reis,
Profer lumen caecis,
Mala nostra pelle,
Bona cuncta posce.

4 Monstra te esse matrem,
Sumat per te preces,
Qui pro nobis natus,
Tulit esse tuus.

5 Virgo Singularis,
Inter omnes mitis,
Nos culpis solutos,
Mites fac et castos.

6 Vitam praesta puram,
Iter para tutum,
Ut videntes Jesum,
Semper collaetemur.

7 Sit laus Deo Patri,
   Summo Christo decus,
   Spiritui Sancto,
   Tribus honor unus.

HYMN FOR THE FEASTS OF APOSTLES.

AEterna Christi munera.

THE Lord's eternal gifts,
   Th' Apostles' mighty praise,
Their Victories, and high reward,
   Sing we in joyful lays.

Lords of the Churches they;
   Triumphant Chiefs of war;
Brave Soldiers of the Heavenly Court;
   True lights for evermore.

Theirs was the Saints' high Faith;
   And quenchless Hope's pure glow;
And perfect Charity, which laid
   The world's fell tyrant low.

In them the Father shone;
   In them the Son o'ercame;
In them the Holy Spirit wrought,
   And fill'd their hearts with flame.

To God, the Father, Son,
   And Spirit, glory be;
As was, and is, and shall be so,
   Through all eternity.

FOR THE FEASTS OF APOSTLES AND EVANGELISTS.

Exultet orbis gaudiis.

Now let the earth with joy resound,
And highest Heaven re-echo round;
Nor Heaven nor earth too high can raise
The great Apostles' glorious praise.

O ye who, throned in glory dread,
Shall judge the living and the dead!
Lights of the world for evermore!
To you the suppliant prayer we pour.

Ye close the sacred gates on high;
At your command apart they fly:
Oh! loose us from the guilty chain
We strive to break, and strive in vain.

Sickness and health your voice obey;
At your command they go or stay;
Oh, then from sin our souls restore;
Increase our virtues more and more.

So when the world is at its end,
And Christ to judgment shall descend,
May we be call'd those joys to see
Prepared from all eternity.

Praise to the Father, with the Son,
And Holy Spirit, Three in One;
As ever was in ages past,
And shall be so while ages last.

FOR THE FEASTS OF MARTYRS.

Deus tuorum militum.

O THOU, of all thy warriors, Lord,
Thyself the crown, and sure reward;
Set us from sinful fetters free,
Who sing thy Martyr's victory.

In selfish pleasures' worldly round
The taste of bitter gall he found;
But Sweet to him was thy blest Name,
And thus to heavenly joys he came.

Right manfully his cross he bore,
And ran his race of torments sore:
For Thee he pour'd his life away;
With Thee he lives in endless day.

We, then, before Thee bending low,
Entreat Thee, Lord, thy love to show
On this the day thy Martyr died,
Who in thy Saints art glorified!

Now to the Father, and the Son,
Be glory while the ages run;
The same, O Holy Ghost! to Thee,
Through ages of eternity.

FOR THE FEASTS OF CONFESSORS.

Iste Confessor Domini, colentes.

1 THE Confessor of Christ, from shore to shore
    Honor'd with solemn rite;
This day went up with joy, his labors o'er,
    To his blest seat in light.

[If it be not the day of his death,
the following is substituted.]

This day receives that homage which is his,
    High in the realms of light.

2 Holy and innocent were all his ways;
    Sweet, temperate, unstain'd;
His life was prayer, — his every breath was praise,
    While breath to him remain'd.

3 Ofttimes his merits high in every land
    In cures have been display'd;
And still does health return at his command
    To many a frame decay'd.

4 Therefore to him triumphant praise we pay
    And yearly songs renew;
Praying our glorious Saint for us to pray,
    All the long ages through.

5 To God, of all the centre and the source,
    Be power and glory given;
Who sways the mighty world through all its course,
    From the bright throne of Heaven.

1 ISTE Confessor Domini, colentes
   Quem pie laudant populi per orbem,
   Hac die laetus meruit beatas
     Scandere sedes.

[Si non est dies obitus, dicatur.]

Hac die laetus meruit supremos
    Laudis honores.

2 Qui pius, prudens, humilis, pudicus,
   Sobriam duxit sine labe vitam,

Donec humanos animavit aurae
　　　　　Spiritus artus.

3　Cujus ob praestans meritum frequentur,
　　AEgra quae passim jacuere membra,
　　Viribus morbi domitis, saluti
　　　　Restituuntur.

4　Noster hinc illi chorus obsequentem
　　Concinit laudem, celebresque palmas;
　　Ut piis ejus precibus juvemur
　　　　Omne per aevum.

5　Sit salus illi, decus atque virtus,
　　Qui super coeli solio coruscans,
　　Totius mundi seriem gubernat
　　　　Trinus et unus.

FOR THE FEASTS OF VIRGINS.

Jesu corona Virginum.

THOU Crown of all the Virgin choir!
　　That holy Mother's Virgin Son!
Who is, alone of womankind,
　　Mother and Virgin both in one;

Encircled by thy Virgin band,
　　Amid the lilies Thou art found;
For thy pure brides with lavish hand
　　Scattering immortal graces round.

And still, wherever Thou dost bend
　　Thy lovely steps, O glorious King,
Virgins upon thy steps attend,
　　And hymns to thy high glory sing.

Keep us, O Purity divine,
> From every least corruption free;
Our every sense from sin refine,
> And purify our souls for Thee.

To God the Father, and the Son,
> All honor, glory, praise, be given;
With Thee, O holy Paraclete!
> Henceforth by all in earth and Heaven.

HYMNS AT THE BENEDICTION OF THE BLESSED SACRAMENT.

O salutaris Hostia.

1 O SAVING Victim! opening wide
> The gate of Heaven to man below!
Our foes press on from every side; —
> Thine aid supply, thy strength bestow.

2 To thy great Name be endless praise,
> Immortal Godhead, One in Three!
Oh, grant us endless length of days,
> In our true native land, with Thee!

> 1 O SALUTARIS Hostia!
> Quae coeli pandis ostium:
> Bella premunt hostilia:
> Da robur, fer auxilium.

> 2 Uni trinoque Domino,
> Sit sempiterna gloria:
> Qui vitam sine termino,
> Nobis donet in patria.

Pange lingua gloriosi.

1 SING, my tongue, the Saviour's glory,
    Of his Flesh the mystery sing:
Of the Blood, all price exceeding,
    Shed by our immortal King,
Destined, for the world's redemption,
    From a noble womb to spring.

2 Of a pure and spotless Virgin
    Born for us on earth below,
He, as Man with man conversing,
    Stay'd, the seeds of truth to sow;
Then He closed in solemn order
    Wondrously his life of woe.

3 On the night of that Last Supper,
    Seated with his chosen band,
He the paschal victim eating,
    First fulfils the law's command;
Then, as Food to all his brethren
    Gives Himself with his own hand.

4 Word made Flesh, the bread of nature
    By his word to Flesh He turns;
Wine into his Blood He changes: —
    What though sense no change discerns?
Only be the heart in earnest,
    Faith her lesson quickly learns.

[Tantum ergo sacramentum.]

5 Down in adoration falling,
    Lo! the sacred Host we hail!
Lo! o'er ancient forms departing,
    Newer rites of grace prevail;

Faith, for all defects supplying,
   Where the feeble senses fail.

6 To the Everlasting Father,
   And the Son who reigns on high,
With the Holy Ghost proceeding
   Forth from Each eternally,
Be salvation, honor, blessing,
   Might, and endless majesty.

    1 PANGE lingua gloriosi
      Corporis mysterium,
      Sanguinisque pretiosi,
      Quem in mundi pretium
      Fructus ventris generosi
      Rex effudit gentium.

    2 Nobis datus, nobis natus
      Ex intacta Virgine,
      Et in mundo conversatus,
      Sparso verbi semine,
      Sui moras incolatus
      Miro clausit ordine.

    3 In supremae nocte coenae
      Recumbens cum fratribus,
      Observata lege plene
      Cibis in legalibus,
      Cibum turbae duodenae
      Se dat suis manibus.

    4 Verbum caro, panem verum
      Verbo carnem efficit:
      Fitque sanguis Christi merum:
      Et, si sensus deficit,

    Ad firmandum cor sincerum
    Sola fides sufficit.

5 Tantum ergo Sacramentum
    Veneremur cernui:
    Et antiquum documentum
    Novo cedat ritui:
    Praestet fides supplementum
    Sensuum defectui.

6 Genitori, Genitoque
    Laus et jubilatio,
    Salus, honor, virtus quoque,
    Sit et benedictio:
    Procedenti ab utroque
    Compar sit laudatio.

Ave, verum corpus natum.

HAIL to Thee! true Body, sprung
From the Virgin Mary's womb!
The same that on the Cross was hung,
And bore for man the bitter doom!

Thou, whose side was pierced, and flow'd
Both with water and with blood;
Suffer us to taste of Thee,
In our life's last agony.

O kind, O loving One!
O Sweet Jesu, Mary's Son!

Adoro Te devote latens Deitas.

O GODHEAD hid, devoutly I adore Thee,
Who truly art within the forms before me;
To Thee my heart I bow with bended knee,
As failing quite in contemplating Thee.

Sight, touch, and taste in Thee are each deceived;
The ear alone most safely is believed;
I believe all the Son of God has spoken,
Than truth's own word there is no truer token.

God only on the Cross lay hid from view;
But here lies hid at once the Manhood too:
And I, in both professing my belief,
Make the same prayer as the repentant thief.

Thy wounds, as Thomas saw, I do not see:
Yet Thee confess my Lord and God to be;
Make me believe Thee ever more and more;
In Thee my hope, in Thee my love to store.

O thou Memorial of our Lord's own dying!
O living Bread, to mortals life supplying!
Make Thou my soul henceforth on Thee to live;
Ever a taste of heavenly sweetness give.

O loving Pelican! O Jesu, Lord!
Unclean I am, but cleanse me in thy blood;
Of which a single drop, for sinners spilt,
Can purge the entire world from all its guilt.

Jesu! whom for the present veil'd I see,
What I so thirst for, oh, vouchsafe to me:
That I may see thy countenance unfolding,
And may be blest thy glory in beholding.

[The following is usually sung after every stanza.]

Jesu, eternal Shepherd! hear our cry;
Increase the faith of all whose souls on
    Thee rely.

JESUS OUR REDEEMER.

Jesu nostra Redemptio.

O JESU! our Redemption!
    Loved and desired with tears!
God, of all worlds Creator!
    Man, in the close of years!

What wondrous pity moved Thee
    To make our cause thine own!
And suffer death and torments,
    For sinners to atone!

O Thou, who piercing Hades,
    Thy captives didst unchain!
Who gloriously ascendedst
    Thy Father's Throne again!

Subdue our many evils
    By mercy all divine;
And comfort with thy presence
    The hearts that for Thee pine.

Be Thou our joy, O Jesu!
    In whom our prize we see;
Always, through all the ages,
    In Thee our glory be.

THE DAY OF JUDGMENT.

Dies irae, dies illa.

NIGHER still, and still more nigh
Draws the Day of Prophecy,
Doom'd to melt the earth and sky.

Oh, what trembling there shall be,
When the world its Judge shall see,
Coming in dread majesty!

Hark! the trump, with thrilling tone,
From sepulchral regions lone,
Summons all before the throne:

Time and Death it doth appal,
To see the buried ages all
Rise to answer at the call.

Now the books are open spread;
Now the writing must be read,
Which condemns the quick and dead

Now, before the Judge severe
Hidden things must all appear;
Naught can pass unpunish'd here.

What shall guilty I then plead?
Who for me will intercede,
When the Saints Shall comfort need?

King of dreadful Majesty!
Who dost freely justify;
Fount of Pity, save Thou me!

Recollect, O Love divine!
'Twas for this lost sheep of thine
Thou thy glory didst resign:

Satest wearied seeking me;
Sufferedst upon the Tree;
Let not vain thy labor be.

Judge of Justice, hear my prayer!
Spare me, Lord, in mercy spare!
Ere the Reckoning-day appear.

Lo! thy gracious face I seek;
Shame and grief are on my cheek;
Sighs and tears my sorrow speak.

Thou didst Mary's guilt forgive;
Didst the dying thief receive;
Hence doth hope within me live.

Worthless are my prayers, I know;
Yet, oh, cause me not to go
Into everlasting woe.

Sever'd from the guilty band,
Make me with thy sheep to stand,
Placing me on thy right hand.

When the cursed in anguish flee
Into flames of misery;
With the Blest then call Thou me.

Suppliant in the dust I lie;
My heart a cinder, crush'd and dry;
Help me, Lord, when death is nigh!

Full of tears, and full of dread
Is the day that wakes the dead,
Calling all, with solemn blast,
From the ashes of the past.

Lord of mercy! Jesu blest!
Grant the Faithful light and rest.

HYMNS
FOR PARTICULAR OCCASIONS OF DEVOTION.

HYMNS FOR COMMUNION.

Ecce Panis Angelorum. (see page 54)

Viva, viva, Gesù. (see page 32)

HYMN OF ST. FRANCIS XAVIER.

O Deus, ego amo Te. (see page 39)

MY GOD AND MY ALL.

"Deus meus et omnia." — St. Francis.

WHILE Thou, O my God, art my help and defender,
No cares can o'erwhelm me, no terrors appal;
The wiles and the snares of this world will but render
More lively my hope in my God and my all.

Yes; Thou art my refuge in sorrow and danger;
My strength when I suffer; my hope when I fall;
My comfort and joy in this land of the stranger;
My treasure, my glory, my God, and my all.

To Thee, dearest Lord, will I turn without ceasing,
Though grief may oppress me, or sorrow befall;
And love Thee, till death, my blest spirit releasing,
Secures to me Jesus, my God and my all.

And when Thou demandest the life Thou hast given,
With joy will I answer thy merciful call;

And quit Thee on earth, but to find Thee in heaven,
My portion forever, my God, and my all.

HOLY COMMUNION.

O WHAT could my Jesus do more,
    Or what greater blessing impart!
O silence, my soul, and Adore,
    And press Him still near to thy heart.

'Tis here from my labors I'll rest,
    Since He makes my poor heart his abode;
To Him all my cares I'll address,
    And speak to the heart of my God.

For life and for death Thou art mine,
    My Saviour, I'm scal'd with thy blood;
Till eternity on me doth shine,
    I'll feed on the flesh of my God.

In Jesus triumphant I live —
    In Jesus exultingly die —
The terrors of death calmly brave —
    In his bosom breathe out my last sigh.

AFTER COMMUNION.

WHAT happiness can equal mine?
    I've found the object of my love —
My Jesus dear — my King divine,
    Is come to me from heaven above!

He chose my heart for his abode;
    There He becomes my daily bread;

There on me flows his healing blood,
    There, with his flesh, my soul is fed.

I am my Love's, and He is mine;
    In me He dwells; in Him I live;
What greater gifts could love combine?
    What greater could even heaven give?

O sacred banquet, heavenly feast!
    O overflowing source of grace!
Where God the food, and man the guest,
    Meet and unite in sweet embrace!

[The Hymns at the Benediction of the Blessed Sacrament, may also be used with advantage.]

FIRST COMMUNION.
HYMN OF ST. BERNARD.

Jesu! dulcis memoria. (see page 22-24)

Lux alma Jesu mentium.

LIGHT of the soul, O Saviour blest!
Soon as thy presence fills the breast,
Darkness and guilt are put to flight,
And all is sweetness and delight.

Son of the Father! Lord most high!
How glad is he who feels Thee nigh!
How Sweet in Heaven thy beam doth glow,
Denied to eye of flesh below!

O Light of Light celestial!
O Charity ineffable!

Come in thy hidden majesty;
Fill us with love, fill us with Thee.

To Jesus, from the proud conceal'd
But evermore to babes reveal'd,
All glory with the Father be,
And Holy Ghost eternally.

LONGING FOR CHRIST.

MY spirit longeth for Thee
    To dwell within my breast;
Although I am unworthy
    Of so divine a Guest!

Of so divine a Guest —
    Unworthy though I be;
Yet hath my heart no rest
    Until it come to Thee!

Until it come to Thee, —
    In vain I look around;
In all that I can see,
    No rest is to be found!

No rest is to be found,
    But in thy bleeding love:
Oh! let my wish be crown'd,
    And send it from above!

Hymns for Confession.

The Sinner's Prayer.

[From the Hymn, Ex more docti mystico.]

Lord! let me shun whatever things
    Distract the erring heart;
And let me shut the soul against
    The tyrant Tempter's art.

Look on these tears, wherewith I strive
    Thy vengeance to appease:
Lord! hear me say with contrite voice,
    Lowly on bended knees:

"Much have I sinn'd, O Lord! and still
    I sin each day I live;
Yet pour thy pity from on high,
    And of thy grace forgive.

Remember that I still am thine,
    Though of a fallen frame:
And take not from me in thy wrath
    The glory of thy name.

Undo past evil; grant me, Lord,
    More grace to do aright;
So let me now and ever find
    Acceptance in thy sight."

Blest Trinity in Unity!
    Vouchsafe me in thy love,
True hate of sin; death in thy grace,
    And endless joys above.

Alma Redemptoris Mater. (see page 8)

Ave Regina coelorum. (see page 8)

Exultet orbis gaudiis. (see page 94)

AFTER CONFESSION

Rex sempiterne coelitum.

O THOU, the Heaven's eternal King!
    Lord of the starry spheres!
Who with the Father equal art
    From everlasting years:

All praise to thy most holy Name,
    Who, when the world began,
Yoking the soul with clay, didst form
    In thine own image, Man.

And praise to Thee, who, when the Foe
    Had marr'd thy work sublime,
Clothing Thyself in flesh, didst mould
    Our race a second time;

When from the tomb new born, as from
    A Virgin born before,
Thou didst reverse our fallen state,
    And life to man restore.

Eternal Shepherd! who thy flock guilt
    In thy pure Font dost lave,
Where souls are cleansed, and all their guilt
    Buried as in a grave;

Jesu! who to the Cross wast nail'd,
    Our countless debt to pay;
Jesu! who lavishly didst pour
    Thy blood for us away:

Oh, from the wretched death of sin
    Keep us; so shalt Thou be
The everlasting Paschal joy
    Of all new born in Thee.

To God the Father, and the Son
    Who rose, be glory given
With Thee, Almighty Paraclete!
    By all in earth and Heaven.

Summi Parentis Unice.

SON of the Highest! deign to cast
    On us a pitying eye;
Thou, who repentant Magdalene
    Didst call to endless joy.

Again the royal treasury
    Receives its long-lost coin;
The gem is found, and, cleansed from mire,
    Doth all the stars outshine.

O Jesu! balm of every wound!
    The sinner's only stay!
Wash Thou in Magdalene's pure tears
    Our guilty spots away.

Mother of God! the sons of Eve
    Weeping thine aid implore:
Oh! land us from the storms of life,
    Safe on th' eternal shore.

Glory, for graces manifold,
    To the one only Lord;
Whose mercy doth our souls forgive,
    Whose bounty doth reward.

HYMNS FOR CONFIRMATION.

Veni Creator Spiritus. (see page 47)

Veni Sancte Spiritus. (see page 49)

OFFERING.

MY God, accept my heart this day,
    And make it always thine,—
That I from Thee no more may stray,
    No more from Thee decline.

Before the cross of Him who died,
    Behold, I prostrate fall:
Let every sin be crucified,—
    Let Christ be all in all!

Anoint me with thy heavenly grace,
    Adopt me for thine own, —
That I may see thy glorious face,
    And worship at thy throne!

May the dear blood, once shed for me,
    My blest atonement prove, —
That I from first to last may be
    The purchase of thy love!

Let every thought, and work and word,
    To Thee be ever given, —

Then life shall be thy service, Lord,
And death the gate of heaven!

HYMNS OF THE LITANY OF OUR LADY.

LADY OF LORETTO.

HAIL, holy Virgin! Mary — Hail!
Whose tender mercies never fail;
Mother of Christ, of grace divine,
Of purity the spotless shrine, —
Mother of God, with virtues crown'd,
Most faithful — pitiful — renown'd;
Deign from thy throne to look on me,
And hear my mournful Litany.

Mirror of justice, and of joy,
Wisdom itself without alloy;
Vessel of honor, and of grace,
Beholding Jesus face to face:
Mystical Rose of rich perfume, —
Beauty of beauties, bathed in bloom:
Deign from thy throne to look on me,
And hear my solemn Litany.

Thou Ivory Tower, beyond compare,
Like that of David, yet more rare;
Palace of peace, and House of Gold,
Ark of the Covenant of old; —
Gate of that heaven beheld afar,
And of dark night the Morning Star:
Deign from thy throne to look on me,
And listen to my Litany.

Health of the weak, to make them strong,
Refuge of sinners, and their song;
Comfort of each afflicted breast,
Haven of hope in realms of rest;—
Queen of the patriarchs gone before,
Light of the prophets' learned lore:
Deign from thy throne to look on me,
And hear my lowly Litany.

Queen of the thousand thousand quires,
Where angels sweep unnumber'd lyres;
Queen of apostles, where they reign
Assessors to the Lamb once slain;
Queen of the martyrs — where they glow
In raiment whiter wash'd than snow;
Queen of all virgins, look on me,
And listen to my Litany.

Lead me, oh! lead me to thy Son,
To taste and feel what He has done;
To lay me low before His cross,
And reckon all besides as dross: —
To speak, and think, and will, and move,
And love, as thou wouldst have me love:
Oh! look upon this bended knee,
And hear my heart's own Litany.

ROSA MYSTICA.

ROSE of the Cross, thou mystic flower!
    I lift my heart to thee:
In every melancholy hour,
    Mary! remember me.

A wanderer here, through many a wild
    Where few their way can see, —

Bloom with thy fragrance on thy child;
    Mary! remember me.

Let me but stand where thou hast stood,
    Beside the crimson tree;
And by the water and the blood,
    Mary! remember me.

There let me wash my sinful soul,
    And be from sin set free;
Drawn by thy love, by grace made whole;
    Mary! remember me.

Be thy blest Son my all in all,
    To whom for life I flee;
And when before His face I fall, —
    Mary! remember me.

Lead me forever to adore
    The glorious One in Three;
And whilst I tremble more and more,
    Mary! remember me.

Rose of the Cross, thou thornless flower,
    May I thy follower be;
And when temptation wields its power,
    Mary! remember me.

TURRIS EBURNEA.

DAUGHTER of David, ever fair,
    In all thy gentle power,
Oh! let me find thy gracious care
    An Ivory Tower!

Created by the King of kings
    To be His own abode, —
Beneath the shadow of His wings,
    Mother of God!

For this to thee in each distress
    As shelter man may run,
And through thee hasten on to bless
    Thy glorious Son.

Defend me then in thine embrace,
    Where safety blends with rest,
To make my paradise of grace
    Thy virgin breast.

Beauty of women! Matchless Maid!
    Immaculate, sublime:
When death in lowly dust hath laid
    All towers of time, —

Thy light impearl'd in bliss shall glow,
    And I will look to thee, —
For thou hast been, in weal and woe,
    A Tower to me.

FOEDERIS ARCA.

HOLY of holies! rend the veil
    Before thy throne of gold:
Ark of the Covenant, all hail, —
    The Virgin we behold!

Bright cherubim and seraphim,
    In one mysterious crowd,

Expand the everlasting hymn
    That rolls from cloud to cloud.

Odors, in folds of fragrant fumes,
    Pervade the ravish'd skies;
Whilst angels form, with arching plumes,
    A firmament of eyes![4]

They gaze, and as they gaze, they shine,
    And as they shine, admire,
With adoration all divine, —
    All love, — all life, — all fire!

No temple there is made with hands
    By human priesthood trod;
Alone the once-slain Victim stands,
    The living Lamb of God!

To Him the Blessed Mary prays,
    With Him she intercedes;
The Church, around her, homage pays,
    For whom her mercy pleads.

Oh! that on earth we yet may bear
    A part with those above;
And mingling oft in spirit there,
    Be swallow'd up of love.

JANUA COELI.

GATE of immortal bliss, —
    Whose sweet celestial ray

---

[4] Ezech. i. 8-23; x. 12: Apocal. iv. 8.

Comes shining o'er the vast abyss,
    That severs night from day, —

My soul unfurls her wings
    To soar aloft to thee, —
And far removed from earthly things,
    Adores thy mystery.

The prophet saw that fane
    Of heavenly beauty fair,
Where Deity itself would deign
    To find a dwelling there:

One portal stood alone,[5]
    Of peerless pearl its frame:
There would the Lord ascend his throne,
    And Mary was its name.

All hail, thou matchless Maid!
    An entrance make for me, —
Where He in glory is display'd
    Who came to us through thee.

By all, and more than mothers know
    In their maternal state, —
By all thy vigils, tears, and woe,
    Thyself immaculate; —

Thou Virgin Queen of earth and heaven,
    Present me to thy Son, —
That every sin may be forgiven,
    And a fresh trophy won.

---

[5] Ezekiel xliv. 1, 2.

STELLA MATUTINA!

STAR of the Morning, like an eye
    That beams upon the brow of love;
Oh! let thy lustrous radiancy
    Shine from above!

Crown of the opening day of days,
    When Jesus as an infant smiled;
Teach every heart aright to praise
    Thy Holy Child!

Brightness of beauty, — Diadem
    Of nature rising out of night;
Lamp of the Church! her Bridal Gem,
    Fountain of Light!

Glory of that celestial zone
    Arranged by God in dread array, —
A galaxy around His throne
    Of saints that pray;

Centre and source of endless grace
    For those who on thee humbly call;
With the bright visions of thy face
    Illumine all!

Star of the Morning, like an eye
    That beams upon the brow of love;
Oh! let thy lustrous radiancy
    Shine from above!

DOMUS AUREA.

LIGHT! Light! Infinite Light!
    The mountains melted away:
Ten thousand thousand seraphim bright
    Were lost in a blaze of day:
For God was there, and beneath His feet
    A pavement of sapphires glow'd,[6]
As the mirror of glory transcendently meet
    To reflect His own abode!

Love! Love! Infinite Love!
    The lowly Lady of grace
Bows underneath the o'ershadowing Dove,
    Her eternal Son to embrace!
For God is there, the Ancient of Days,
    An Infant of human years:
Whilst angels around them incessantly gaze,
    And nature is wrapt in tears!

Peace! Peace! Infinite Peace!
    A Golden House hath it found,
Whose ineffable beauty must ever increase,
    With immortality crown'd!
For God was there, the Lord of the skies,
    Whose loud alleluias ran
From heaven to earth, — as Emmanuel lies
    In the arms of Mary for man!

---

[6] Exodus xxiv. 10.

ALL SAINTS!

HEAD of the Hosts in glory!
We joyfully adore Thee, —
    Thy Church on earth below,
Blending with those on high, —
Where through the azure sky
Thy saints in ecstasy, —
    Forever glow!

Armies of God! in union
With us, through one communion, —
    Pour forth sweet prayers:
Our souls in love embrace,—
Around the Saviour' face, —
And ask His special grace
    To soothe our cares.

Offer those golden vials[7]
Of odors, — for our trials, —
    Before the throne:
Till God the Father smile
On us, — though we were vile, —
Now counted without guile,
    Through Christ alone!

Then raise the song of gladness,
To dissipate our sadness—
    Along this vale of tears;
We wend our weary way
Up towards the realms of day, —
And watch, — and wait, — and pray,
    Constant in fears!

Holy Apostles! — beaming
With radiance brightly streaming

---

[7] Apocalypse, v. 8.

  From diadems of power;
Call on the awful name, —
That we, through flood and flame,
The gospel may proclaim,
  In every hour!

Martyrs! — whose mystic legions
March o'er yon heavenly regions
  In triumph round and round:
Wave — wave your banners — wave!
Your God — our Saviour, clave
For Death itself a grave, —
  In hell profound!

Saints! — in fair circles, casting
Rich trophies everlasting
  At Jesu's pierced feet, —
Amidst our rude alarms,
Stretch forth your conquering arms,
That we, too, safe from harms,
  In heaven may meet!

Virgins! — in bliss transcendent,
Whose coronals resplendent
  Unwithering bloom:
Exalt, in ceaseless lays,
Him whom all anthems praise,
And oft our spirits raise
  With your perfume!

Angels — Archangels! glorious
Guards of the Church victorious!
  Worship the Lamb!
Crown Him with crowns of light, —
One of the Three by right, —
Love, — Majesty, — and Might,—
  The Great I AM!

MONTH OF MAY.
PIOUS ASPIRATIONS TO THE MOTHER OF GOD, FOR EVERY DAY IN THE MONTH.

[From the Italian.]

1. JOY of my heart! O let me pay
   To Thee thine own sweet month of May.

2. Mary! one gift I beg of Thee, —
   My soul from sin and sorrow free.

3. Direct my wandering feet aright,
   And be thyself mine own true light.

4. Be love of Thee the purging fire,
   To cleanse for God my heart's desire.

5. Mother! be love of Thee a ray
   From Heaven, to show the heavenward way.

6. Mary! make haste thy child to win
   From sin, and from the love of sin.

7. Mother of God! let my poor love
   A mother's prayers and pity move.

8. Oh, Mary, when I come to die,
   Be Thou, thy spouse, and Jesus nigh.

9. When mute before the Judge I stand,
   My holy shield be Mary's hand.

10. Oh, Mary! let no child of thine
    In hell's eternal exile pine.

11. If time for penance still be mine,
    Mother, the precious gift is thine.

12. Thou, Mary, art my hope and life,
    The starlight of this earthly strife.

13. Oh, for my own, and others' sin,
    Do Thou, who canst, free pardon win.

14. To sinners all, to me the chief,
    Send, Mother, send thy kind relief.

15. To Thee our love and troth are given;
    Pray for us, pray, bright Gate of Heaven.

16. Sweet Day-Star! let thy beauty be
    A light to draw my soul to Thee.

17. We love Thee, light of sinners' eyes!
    O let thy prayer for sinners rise.

18. Look at us, Mother Mary see
    How piteously we look to Thee.

19. I am thy slave, nor would I be
    For worlds from this sweet bondage free.

20. Oh, Jesus, Joseph, Mary, deign
    My soul in heavenly ways to train.

21. Sweet Stewardess of God, thy prayers
    We beg, who are God's ransom'd heirs.

22. Oh, Virgin born! Oh, Flesh Divine!
    Cleanse us, and make us wholly thine.

23. Mary, dear Mistress of my heart,
    What thou wouldst have me do, impart.

24. Thou, who wert pure as driven snow,
    Make me as Thou wert here below.

25. Oh, Queen of Heaven! obtain for me
    Thy glory there one day to see.

26. O then and there, on that bright day,
    To me thy womb's chaste Fruit display.

27. Mother of God! to me no less
    Vouchsafe a mother's sweet caress.

28. Be love of Thee, my whole life long,
    A seal upon my wayward tongue.

29. Write on my heart's most sacred core
    The five dear wounds that Jesus bore.

30. O give me tears to shed with Thee
    Beneath the Cross on Calvary.

31. One more request, and I have done; —
    With love of Thee and thy dear Son,
    More let me burn, and more each day,
    Till love of self is burn'd away.

CHRISTMAS VESPER HYMN.

DEPART awhile, each thought of care,
    Be earthly things forgotten all!
And speak, my soul, thy vesper prayer,
    Obedient to that sacred call.
For hark! the pealing chorus swells;
    Devotion chants the hymn of praise,
And now of joy and hope it tells,
    Till fainting on the ear, it says,
        Gloria tibi Domine,
        Domine, Domine.

Thine, wondrous Babe of Galilee!
    Fond theme of David's harp and song,
Thine are the notes of minstrelsy —
    To Thee its ransom'd chords belong.
And hark! again the chorus swells,
    The song is wafted on the breeze,
And to the listening earth it tells —
    In accents soft and sweet as these —
        Gloria tibi Domine.

My heart doth feel that still He's near,
    To meet the soul in hours like this,
Else — why, O why that falling tear!
    When all is peace, and love, and bliss!
But hark! that pealing chorus swells
    Anew its thrilling vesper strain;
And still of joy and hope it tells,
    And bids creation sing again,
        Gloria tibi Domine.

Hymn before Prayer, Sermon, Catecism, etc.

Ven Creator Spiritus.

COME, O Creator Spirit!
    Visit this soul of thine;
This heart of thy creating
    Fill Thou with grace divine.

Who Paraclete art call'd!
    The gift of God above!
Pure Unction! holy Fire!
    And Fount of life and love!

Finger of God's right hand!
    The Father's promise true!
Who sevenfold gifts bestowest!
    Who dost the tongue endow!

Pour love into our hearts;
    Our senses touch with light;
Make strong our human frailty
    With thy supernal might.

Cast far our deadly Foe;
    Thy peace in us fulfil;
So, Thee before us leading,
    May we escape each ill.

The Father, and the Son,
    Through Thee may we receive;
In Thee, from Both proceeding,
    Through endless time believe.

Praise to the Father be;
    Praise to the Son who rose;
And praise to Thee, blest Spirit!
    While age on ages flows.

FOR AID IN PRAYER.
ANOTHER HYMN BEFORE PRAYER, ETC.

DEAR Lord! prepare our souls, and train
    Our hearts in thoughts of love to pray;
Teach us to know our sins, and gain
    New triumphs o'er ourselves each day.

How oft our thoughts, in idle chase,
    On vanity and sin run wild,
Our best resolves, in varying phase,
    Beguiling come, or go beguiled!

Scarce have we thought on good, and vow'd
    Firmly to walk in virtue's road,
Than various lures around us crowd,
    And push aside the needful goad.

Caught by a glittering bait, we fall
    Sin's easy, weak, and thoughtless prey;
While, all unheeded, virtue's call
    Beckons in vain another way.

Alas! dear Lord, for we are weak,
    Without thy help, alas! for hell!—
Oh! hear us, then! In mercy, speak!
    And teach us all our foes to quell.

Dear Lord, Thou hast full often said,
    There is a path — one only way —
Oh! come, then, quickly to our aid,
    And teach us how and what to pray.

Hymn before Singing.

Nunc sancte nobis Spiritus.

Come, Holy Ghost, and through each heart
    In thy full flood of glory pour;
Who, with the Son and Father, art
    One Godhead blest for evermore.

So shall voice, mind, and strength conspire
    Thy praise eternal to resound;
So shall our hearts be set on fire,
    And kindle every heart around.

Father of mercies! hear our cry!
    Hear us, O sole-begotten Son!
Who, with the Holy Ghost most high,
    Reignest while endless ages run.

Hymn before Family Prayer.

Summae Parens clementiae.

O Thou eternal Source of love!
    Ruler of nature's scheme!
In Substance One in Persons Three!
    Omniscient and Supreme!

For thy dear mercy's sake receive
    The strains and tears we pour,
And purify our hearts to taste
    Thy sweetness more and more.

Our flesh, our reins, our spirits, Lord,
    In thy clear fire refine;

Break down the self-indulgent will;
    Gird us with strength divine.

So may all we, who here are met
    This night[8] thy name to bless,
One day, in our eternal home,
    Thine endless joys possess.

Father of mercies! hear our cry;
    Hear us, coequal Son!
Who reignest with the Holy Ghost
    While ceaseless ages run.

OUR GREAT PROTECTOR.

THE Lord himself, the mighty God,
    Vouchsafes to be my guide,
The Shepherd by whose constant care
    My wants are all supplied.

In verdant meads he makes me feed,
    And gently there repose;
Then leads me to cool shades, and where
    Refreshing water flows.

He does my wandering soul reclaim,
    And, to his endless praise,
Instructs with humble zeal to walk
    In his most righteous ways.

I pass the gloomy vale of death,
    From fear and danger free,
For there his aiding rod and staff
    Defend and comfort me.

---

[8] For family prayers in the morning, instead of "This night," say "This morn."

In presence of my spiteful foes,
    He does my table spread;
He crowns my cup with cheerful wine,
    With oil anoints my head.

Since God doth thus his wondrous love
    Through all my life extend,
That life to Him I will devote,
    And in His temple spend.

CHILDREN OF THE HEAVENLY KING.

CHILDREN of the Heavenly King,
As we journey, let us sing;
Sing our Saviour's worth and praise,
Glorious in His works and ways.

We are travelling home to God,
In the way the fathers trod;
They are happy now, and we
Soon their happiness shall see.

O ye banish'd seed, be glad,
Christ our Advocate is made
Us to save, our flesh assumes,
Brother to our souls becomes.

Lord, obediently we go,
Gladly leaving all below;
Only Thou our leader be,
And we still will follow Thee.

PRAISES TO THE LORD.

SING ye praises to the Lord, Alleluia,
Bless his name with one accord, Alleluia,
For 'tis owing to His care, Alleluia,
What we have, and what we are, Alleluia.

He first made us by His power, Alleluia,
He preserves us ev'ry hour, Alleluia,
Food and raiment all are His, Alleluia,
Present comfort, future bliss, Alleluia.

He directs our steps by day, Alleluia,
Pointing out the safest way, Alleluia,
And at night in mercy still, Alleluia,
Guards us from all kinds of ill, Alleluia.

God forgave us when undone, Alleluia,
And redeem'd us by his Son, Alleluia:
Raise your voices then, and sing, Alleluia,
Loud hosannas to our King, Alleluia.

CHILD'S PRAYER.

O LORD! another day is flown;
    And we, a humble band,
Lift up our voice before thy throne,
    To bless thy fost'ring hand.
And wilt Thou lend a list'ning ear
    To praises such as ours?
Thou wilt; for Thou dost love to hear
    The song which childhood pours.

Through thy dear Son we now address
    Our prayer to Thee above;

For He did little children bless
    With words and looks of love.
O Father! guide our wand'ring feet,
    And bless us on our way,
Until at length with joy we greet
    The dawn of endless day.

ST. VINCENT OF PAUL.

July 19.

MILD and serene, ye angels appear;
    Assist us with your heavenly power
To sing his praise, whom to-day we revere:
    On thee we call, St. Vincent of Paul:
        Aid and protect us;
        May we from thee
        Learn blest charity
        Holy Patron, hear our prayer.

In thy blest bosom all virtues reign'd:
    Thou wert the helpless orphan's father,
Thou wert the cheerless widow's friend,
    And slavery, comforted by thee,
        Found peace in its fetters.
        May we, &c.

Youth and old age from thee found relief,
    Oft by zealous endeavors reclaiming
The sinner from vice, to a contrite return;
    Thus you restored to its Master and Lord
        The soul that was straying.
        May we, &c.

Teach us thy lessons of grace to improve;
    Still more and more in our bosoms increasing,

Life shall pass on in our Jesus's love,
Till we with thee in eternity
Will adore Him forever.
May we. &c.

HYMN TO ST. ALOYSIUS GONZAGA.

June 21.

THE youth who wealth and courts despised,
His spotless mind above to raise,
Who every rising thought chastised —
'Tis Aloysius claims our lays.

CHORUS.

Amiable and angelic youth,
Aloysius, pray for us.

Born by the sacred Virgin's aid,
Soon as his eyes the light could view,
His soul the heir of heaven was made,
By the renovating dew.
Amiable, &c.

His infant words, the first he frames,
He utters with a trembling voice:
Jesus and Mary! hallow'd names,
Dwell on his lips, and speak his choice.
Amiable, &c.

Charm'd with the Deity alone,
Terrestrial pursuits he forsakes,
And ere yet half to manhood grown,
His virgin vows to Mary makes.
Amiable, &c.

The tenor of his life so bright,
    So full of Angel purity,
A seraph from the realms of light,
    Dwelling on earth, he seem'd to be.
    Amiable, &c.

No titles win nor honors move,
    No worldly charms his mind allure;
The ties of blood but serve to prove
    His soul on every side secure.
    Amiable, &c.

Enamor'd of celestial joys,
    Let pride and wealth my choice withstand;
I scorn their gifts, they are but toys,
    He said, and joins Loyola's band.
    Amiable, &c.

To gain perfection's utmost height,
    He tries, nor was his trial vain;
Of sanctity a model bright,
    He stands a mirror clear of stain.
    Amiable, &c.

To Jesus' venerable name
    May endless love and praise accrue;
To blessed Trinity the same;
    To Aloysius honor due.
    Amiable, &c.

HYMN TO ST. STANISLAUS KOTSKA.

May 7.

O YE angelic bands, attend!
    From heaven's high exalted spires,
With mortal accents, deign to blend
    The voice of your harmonious choirs.

In early life's most tender state,
    (O thy designs, how great, O God!)
Young Stanislaus could emulate
    The virtuous paths that saints have trod.

Thy tenderness, O Virgin bright,
    Places within his youthful arms
The object of his soul's delight,
    An infant Saviour's lovely charms.

Oh happiness supremely great!
    No grandeur can his heart decoy
Jesus, thy order grants a seat,
    Receives the youth, and crowns his joy.

Deluding world, thy threats are vain,
    Your tinsel pleasures lose their charms;
The generous youth they can't detain,
    He lives secure in Jesus' arms.

In joyful strains come sound his praise,
    With anthems fill the vaulted sky;
Ye angels, wake your choicest lays,
    And greet the saint now flown on high.

HYMN TO ST. CECILIA.

November 22.

LET the deep organ swell the lay,
In honor of this festive day,
And let harmonious choirs proclaim
Cecilia's ever-blessed name.

Rome gave the Virgin martyr birth,
Whose memory has fill'd the earth,
Who, in the early dawn of youth,
Has fix'd her heart on God and truth:

Thence from the world's bewild'ring strife,
In peace she spent her holy life,
Teaching the organ to combine
With voice to praise the Lamb divine

When bade forthwith her faith deny,
And with the pagan rites comply,
She nobly chose the bath of fire,
There to be tortured and expire:

But there the Virgin felt no pain:
One night and day she did remain,
When, roused by vengeance, with a blow,
The lictor laid the Martyr low.

Cecilia, with a twofold crown
Adorn'd in heaven, we pray, look down
Upon thy pious vot'ries here,
And hearken to their humble prayer.

HYMN TO ST. FRANCIS XAVIER.

December 3.

WITH grateful hearts, let's all combine,
    And sing to-day our choicest lays;
Let's all in tuneful accents join,
    To sound the great Xaverius' praise.

Xaverius, great Loyola's son,
    By words divine from error gain'd,
By fervor soon the conquest won —
    The earth once loved, he soon disdain'd.

With toils immense, both sea and land,
    Immortal souls to God to gain,
He measures o'er at God's command,
    Then dies upon a desert plain.

HYMN TO OUR BLESSED LADY,
FOR THE SOULS IN PURGATORY.

O TURN to Jesus, Mother! turn,
    And call Him by his tenderest names;
Pray for the Holy Souls that burn
    This hour amid the cleansing flames.

Ah! they have fought a gallant fight;
    In death's cold arms they persevered;
And after life's uncheery night,
    The harbor of their rest is near'd.

In pains beyond all earthly pains,
    Favorites of Jesus! there they lie,
Letting the fire wear out their stains,
    And worshipping God's purity.

Spouses of Christ they are, for He
    Was wedded to them by his blood;
The faithful Cross their trysting-tree,
    Their marriage-bed its hallow'd wood.

They are the children of thy tears;
    Then hasten, Mother! to their aid;
In pity think each hour appears
    An age while glory is delay'd.

See, how they bound amid their fires,
    While pain and love their spirits fill;
Then with self-crucified desires
    Utter sweet murmurs, and lie still.

Ah me! the love of Jesus yearns
    O'er that abyss of sacred pain,
And as He looks, his bosom burns
    With Calvary's dear thirst again.

O Mary! let thy Son no more
    His lingering Spouses thus expect;
God's children to their God restore,
    And to the Spirit his elect.

Pray, then, as thou hast ever pray'd;
    Angels and, Souls all look to thee;
God waits thy prayers, for He hath made
    Those prayers his law of charity.

HYMN TO MY GUARDIAN ANGEL.

FOR CHILDREN.

DEAR Angel! ever at my side,
    How loving must thou be,
To leave thy home in Heaven to guard
    A little child like me!

Thy beautiful and shining face
    I see not, though so near;
The sweetness of thy soft low voice
    I am too deaf to hear.

I cannot feel thee touch my hand
    With pressure light and mild,
To check me, as my mother did
    When I was but a child.

But I have felt thee in my thoughts
    Fighting with sin for me;
And when my heart loves God, I know
    The sweetness is from thee.

And when, dear Spirit! I kneel down
    Morning and night to prayer,
Something there is within my heart
    Which tells me thou art there.

Yes! when I pray thou prayest too —
    Thy prayer is all for me;
But when I sleep, thou sleepest not,
    But watchest patiently.

But most of all I feel thee near,
    When, from the good priest's feet,

I go absolved, in fearless love,
    Fresh toils and cares to meet.

And thou in life's last hour wilt bring
    A fresh supply of grace,
And afterwards wilt let me kiss
    Thy beautiful bright face.

Ah me! how lovely they must be
    Whom God has glorified!
Yet one of them, O sweetest thought!
    Is ever at my side.

Then for thy sake, dear Angel! now
    More humble will I be:
But I am weak, and when I fall,
    O weary not of me;

O weary not, but love me still,
    For Mary's sake, thy Queen;
She never tired of me, though I
    Her worst of sons have been.

She will reward thee with a smile;
    Thou know'st what it is worth!
For Mary's smiles each day convert
    The hardest hearts on earth.

Then love me, love me, Angel dear!
    And I will love thee more;
And help me when my soul is cast
    Upon the eternal shore.

FOR A HAPPY DEATH.

"Moriatur anima mea morte justorum."
Numb. xxxiii. 10.

WHILST I dwell, O my God, in this valley of tears,
    For refuge and comfort I fly unto Thee;
And when death's awful hour with its terror appears,
    O merciful Jesus, have mercy on me.

When my soul, on the verge of its final release,
    By the shadows of death o'erclouded shall be;
When earthly enjoyments forever shall cease,
    Thou, Joy of the Dying, bring mercy to me.

When my strength shall decline, and my anguish increase,
    And my sins beyond number with terror I'll see;
When I turn to thy mercy for pardon and peace,
    Then, Hope of the Sinner, beam brightly on me.

When weaken'd by illness — by terror oppress'd,
    My pains and my terrors I offer to Thee;
When vainly I seek for some solace or rest,
    Then, Strength of the Martyrs, bring comfort to me.

When my reason shall fail, and my life shall decay;
    When the scenes of this world shall vanish and flee;
When sunshine and shower alike pass away,
    Then, Light of the Blessed, shine sweetly on me.

When heedless of earth, and of all that surround me,
    For pardon and mercy I'll call upon Thee;
When death with its fetters forever has bound me,
    Then Jesus, — sweet Jesus, — be Jesus to me.

When, weeping, my friends shall with fervor implore Thee,
    My strength, my protector, my succor to be;

When, helpless and lonely, I tremble before Thee,
    Then, Fountain of Mercy, have mercy on me.

Then, dear Lord, the dark chain of my mis'ries sever;
    Then, Rest of the Weary-one, call me to Thee;
Then, Crown of the Just, be my portion forever;
    Then, merciful Jesus, have mercy on me.

THE MOST HOLY TRINITY.

HAVE mercy on us, God Most High!
    Have mercy upon me,
Have mercy on us worms of earth,
    Most Holy Trinity!

Most ancient of all mysteries!
    Before thy throne we lie;
Have mercy now, most merciful,
    Most Holy Trinity!

When heaven and earth were yet unmade,
    When time was yet unknown,
Thou in thy bliss and majesty
    Didst live and love alone!

Thou wert not born, there was no fount
    From which thy being flow'd;
There is no end which Thou canst reach;
    But Thou art simply God.

How wonderful creation is,
    The work that Thou didst bless!
And, oh! what then must Thou be like,
    Eternal Loveliness!

How beautiful the Angels are!
    The Saints, how bright in bliss!
But with thy beauty, Lord! compared,
    How dull, how poor is this!

In wonder lost, the highest heavens
    Mary, their queen, may see.
If Mary is so beautiful,
    What must her Maker be?

No wonder Saints have died of love,
    No wonder hearts can break,
Pure hearts that once have learn'd to love
    God for his own dear sake.

O Majesty most beautiful!
    Most Holy Trinity!
On Mary's throne we climb to get
    A far-off sight of Thee.

O listen, then, Most Pitiful!
    To thy poor creature's heart;
It blesses Thee that Thou art God,
    That Thou art what Thou art!

Most ancient of all mysteries!
    Still at thy throne we lie;
Have mercy now, most merciful,
    Most Holy Trinity!

THE INFANT JESUS

DEAR Little One! how sweet Thou art,
    Thine eyes how bright they shine!
So bright they almost seem to speak
    When Mary's look meets thine!

How faint and feeble is thy cry,
    Like plaint of harmless dove,
When Thou dost murmur in thy sleep
    Of sorrow and of love!

When Mary bids Thee sleep, Thou sleep'st,
    Thou wakest when she calls;
Thou art content upon her lap,
    Or in the rugged stalls.

Simplest of Babes! with what a grace
    Thou dost thy Mother's will!
Thine infant fashions well betray
    The Godhead's hidden skill.

When Joseph takes Thee in his arms,
    And smooths thy little cheek,
Thou lookest up into his face
    So helpless and so meek.

Yes! Thou art what Thou seem'st to be,
    A thing of smiles and tears;
Yet Thou art God, and heaven and earth
    Adore Thee with their fears.

Yes! dearest Babe! those tiny hands,
    That play with Mary's hair,
The weight of all the mighty world
    This very moment bear.

While Thou art clasping Mary's neck
    In timid tight embrace,
The boldest seraphs veil themselves
    Before thine infant face.

When Mary hath appeased thy thirst,
    And hush'd thy feeble cry,
The hearts of men lie open still
    Before thy slumbering eye.

Art Thou, weak Babe! my very God?
    O I must love Thee, then;
Love Thee, and yearn to spread thy love
    Among forgetful men.

O dear! O wakeful-hearted Child!
    Sleep on, dear Jesus! sleep;
For Thou must one day wake for me
    To suffer and to weep.

A Scourge, a Cross, a cruel Crown
    Have I in store for Thee;
Yet why? one little tear, O Lord!
    Ransom enough would be.

But no! death is thine own sweet will,
    The price decreed above;
Thou wilt do more than save our souls,
    For Thou wilt die for love.

JESUS CRUCIFIED.

O COME and mourn with me awhile;
    See, Mary calls us to her side;
O come and let us mourn with her, —
    Jesus, our Love, is crucified!

Have we no tears to shed for Him,
    While soldiers scoff and Jews deride?
Ah! look, how patiently He hangs, —
    Jesus, our Love, is crucified!

How fast His hands and feet are nail'd!
    His blessed tongue with thirst is tied,
His failing eyes are blind with blood, —
    Jesus, our Love, is crucified!

His Mother cannot reach his face;
    She stands in helplessness beside;
Her heart is martyr'd with her Son's, —
    Jesus, our Love, is crucified!

Seven times He spoke, seven words of love,
    And all three hours His silence cried
For mercy on the souls of men; —
    Jesus, our Love, is crucified!

What was thy crime, my dearest Lord?
    By earth, by heaven, Thou hast been tried,
And guilty found of too much love; —
    Jesus, our Love, is crucified!

Found guilty of excess of love,
    It was thine own sweet will that tied
Thee tighter far than helpless nails; —
    Jesus, our Love, is crucified!

Death came, and Jesus meekly bow'd;
    His falling eyes He strove to guide
With mindful love to Mary's face; —
    Jesus, our Love, is crucified!

O break, O break, hard heart of mine!
    Thy weak self-love and guilty pride
His Pilate and his Judas were; —
    Jesus, our Love, is crucified!

Come, take thy stand beneath the Cross,
    And let the blood from out that side
Fall gently on thee drop by drop; —
    Jesus, our Love, is crucified!

A broken heart, a fount of tears,—
    Ask, and they will not be denied;
A broken heart love's cradle is;—
    Jesus, our Love, is crucified!

O Love of God! O Sin of Man!
    In this dread act your strength is tried;
And victory remains with love,
    For He, our Love, is crucified!

THE ASCENSION.

WHY is thy face so lit with smiles,
    Mother of Jesus! why?
And wherefore is thy beaming look
    So fix'd up on the sky?

From out thine overflowing eyes
    Bright lights of gladness part,
As though some gushing fount of joy
    Had broken in thy heart.

Mother! how canst thou smile to-day?
    How can thine eyes be bright,
When He, thy Life, thy Love, thine All,
    Hath vanish'd from thy sight?

His rising form on Olivet
    A summer's shadow cast;
The branches of the hoary trees
    Droop'd a s the shadow pass'd.

And as He rose with all his train
    Of righteous souls around,
His blessing fell into thine heart,
    Like dew into the ground.

Down stoop'd a silver cloud from heaven,
    The Eternal Spirit's car,
And on the lessening vision went,
    Like some receding star.

The silver cloud hath sail'd away,
    The skies are blue and free;
The road that vision took is now
    Sunshine and vacancy.

The feet which thou hast kiss'd so oft,
    Those living feet, are gone;
Mother! thou canst but stoop and kiss
    Their print upon the stone.

He loved the Flesh thou gavest Him,
    Because it was from thee;
He loved it, for it gave Him power
    To bleed and die for me.

That Flesh with its five witness Wounds
    Unto his throne He bore,
For God to love, and spirits blest
    To worship evermore.

Yes! He hath left thee, Mother dear!
    His throne is far above;
How canst thou be so full of joy
    When thou hast lost thy Love?

O surely earth's poor sunshine now
    To thee mere gloom appears,
When He is gone who was its light
    For three-and-thirty years.

Why do not thy sweet hands detain
    His feet upon their way?
O why doth not the Mother speak,
    And bid her Son to stay?

Ah no! thy love is rightful love,
    From all self-seeking free;
The change that is such gain to Him
    Can be no loss to thee!

'Tis sweet to feel our Saviour's love,
    To feel his presence near;
Yet loyal love his glory holds
    A thousand times more dear.

Who would have known the way to love
    Our Jesus as we ought,
If thou in varied joy and woe
    Hadst not that lesson taught?

Ah! never is our love so pure
    As when refined by pain,
Or when God's glory upon earth
    Finds in our loss its gain!

True love is worship: Mother dear!
    O gain for us the light
To love, because the creature's love
    Is the Creator's right!

THE MISSION OF THE HOLY GHOST.

No track is on the sunny sky,
    No footprints on the air;
Jesus hath gone; the face of earth
    Is desolate and bare.

The blessed feet of Mary's Son,
    They tread the streets no more;
His soul-converting voice gives not
    Its music as before.

His Mother sits all worshipful
    With her majestic mien;
The princes of the infant Church
    Are gather'd round their Queen.

They gaze on her with raptured eyes,
    Her features are like His,
Her presence is their ample strength,
    Her face reflects their bliss.

That Upper Room is heaven on earth;
    Within its precincts lie
All that earth has of faith, or hope,
    Or heaven-born charity.

The eye of God looks down on them,
    His love is centred there;
His Spirit yearns to be o'ercome
    By their sweet strife of prayer.

The Mother prays her mighty prayer,
    In accents meek and faint,
And highest heaven is quick to own
    The beautiful constraint.

The Eternal Son takes up the prayer
    Upon His royal throne;
The Son his human Mother hears,
    The Sire his equal Son.

The Spirit hears, and He consents
    His mission to fulfil;
For what is ask'd hath ever been
    His own eternal will.

Ten days and nights in acts divine
    Of awful love were spent,
While Mary and her children pray'd
    The Spirit might be sent.

The joy of angels grew and grew
    On Mary's wondrous prayer,
And the Divine Complacence stoop'd
    To feed His glory there.

Her eyes to heaven were humbly raised,
    While for her Spouse she pray'd;
Methought the sweetness of her prayer
    His blissful coming stay'd.

Forever coming did He seem,
    Forever on the wing;
His chosen angels round His throne
    Now gazed, now ceased to sing.

How beautiful, how passing speech,
    The Dove did then appear,
As the hour of His humility
    At Mary's word drew near!

The hour was come; the wings of love
    By His own will were freed:
The hour was come; the Eternal Three
    His mission had decreed.

Then for His love of worthless men,
    His love of Mary's worth,
His beauteous wings the Dove outspread,
    And wing'd his flight to earth.

O wondrous Flight! He left not heaven,
    Though earth's low fields He won,
But in the Bosom still reposed
    Of Father and of Son.

O Flight! O blessed Flight of love!
    Let me thy mercies share;
Grant it, sweet Dove! for my poor soul
    Was part of Mary's prayer!

THE DESCENT OF THE HOLY GHOST.

O MIGHTY Mother! why that light
    In thine uplifted eye?
Why that resplendent lo ok of more
    Than queenlike majesty?

O waitest thou in this thy joy
    For Gabriel once again?
Is heaven about to part, and make
    The Blessed Vision plain?

She sat; beneath her shadow were
    The Chosen of her Son;
Within each heart and on each face
    Her power and spirit shone.

Hers was the courage they had won
    From her prevailing prayers;
They gazed on her, until her heart
    Began to beat in theirs.

Her Son had left that heart to them:
    For ten long nights and days,
The Saviour gone, no Spirit come,
    She ruled their infant ways.

Queen of the Church! around thee shines
    The purest light of heaven,
And all created things to thee
    For thy domain are given!

Why waitest thou then so abash'd,
    Wrapt in ecstatic fear,
Speechless with adoration, hush'd, —
    Hush'd as though God were near?

She is a creature! See! she bows,
    She trembles though so great; —
Created Majesty o'erwhelm'd
    Before the Increate!

He comes! He comes! that mighty Breath
    From heaven's eternal shores;
His uncreated freshness fills
    His Bride as she adores.

Earth quakes before that rushing blast,
    Heaven echoes back the sound,
And mightily the tempest wheels
    That Upper Room around.

One moment — and the silentness
    Was breathless as the grave;
The flutter'd earth forgot to quake,
    The troubled trees to wave.

One moment— and the Spirit hung
    O'er her with dread desire;
Then broke upon the heads of all
    In cloven tongues of fire.

Who knows in what a sea of love
    Our Lady's heart He drown'd?
Or what new gifts He gave her then?
    What ancient gifts He crown'd?

Grace was so multiplied on her,
    So grew within her heart,
She stands alone, earth's miracle,
    A being all apart.

What gifts He gave those chosen men
    Past ages can display;
Nay more, their vigor still inspires
    The weakness of to-day.

Those Tongues still speak within the Church,
    That Fire is undecay'd;
Its well-spring was that Upper Room,
    Where Mary sat and pray'd.

The Spirit came into the Church
    With His unfailing power;
He is the Living Heart that beats
    Within her at this hour.

Speak gently, then, of Church, and Saints,
  Lest you His ways reprove;
The Heart, the Pulses of the Church
  Are God's Eternal Love.

O let us fall and worship Him,
  The Love of Sire and Son,
The Consubstantial Breath of God,
  The Coeternal One!

Ah! see, how like the Incarnate Word,
  His blessed Self He lowers,
To dwell with us invisibly,
  And make His riches ours.

Most humble Spirit! Mighty God!
  Sweet must thy presence be,
If loss of Jesus can be gain,
  So long as we have Thee!

TO OUR BLESSED LADY.

MOTHER of Mercy! day by day
  My love of thee grows more and more;
Thy gifts are strown upon my way
  Like sands upon the great sea shore.

Though poverty, and work, and woe,
  The masters of my life may be,
When times are worst, who does not know
  Darkness is light with love of thee?

But scornful men have coldly said
  Thy love was leading me from God;
And yet in this I did but tread
  The very path my Saviour trod.

They know but little of thy worth
    Who speak these heartless words to me;
For what did Jesus love on earth
    One half so tenderly as thee?

Get me the grace to love thee more;
    Jesus will give if thou wilt plead;
And, Mother! when life's cares are o'er,
    O, I shall love thee then indeed!

Jesus, when His three hours were run,
    Bequeathed thee from the cross to me;
And O! how can I love thy Son,
    Sweet Mother! if I love not thee?

THE ASSUMPTION.

SING, sing, ye Angel Bands,
    All beautiful and bright;
For higher still, and higher,
    Through the vast fields of light,
Mary, your Queen, ascends,
    Like the sweet moon at night.

A fairer flower than she
    On earth hath never been;
And, save the Throne of God,
    Your heavens have never seen
A wonder half so bright
    As your ascending Queen.

O happy Angels! look,
    How beautiful she is!
See! Jesus bears her up,
    Her hand is locked in His;

O who can tell the height
    Of that fair Mother's bliss?

And shall I lose thee, then,
    Lose my sweet right to thee?
Ah! no — the Angels' Queen
    Our mother still will be,
And thou, upon thy throne,
    Wilt keep thy love for me.

THE CREATION OF THE ANGELS.

IN pulses deep of threefold Love,
    Self-hush'd and self-possess'd,
The mighty, unbeginning God
    Had lived in silent rest.

With His own greatness all alone
    The sight of Self had been
Beauty of beauties, joy of joys
    Before His eye serene.

He lay before Himself, and gazed
    As ravish'd with the sight,
Brooding on His own attributes
    With dread untold delight.

No ties were on His bliss, for He
    Had neither end nor cause;
For His own glory 'twas enough
    That He was what He was.

His glory was full grown; His light
    Had own'd no dawning dim;
His love did not outgrow Himself,
    For naught could grow in Him.

He stirr'd — and yet we know not how
    Nor wherefore He should move;
In our poor human words, it was
    An overflow of love.

It was the first outspoken word
    That broke that peace sublime,
An outflow of eternal love
    Into the lap of time.

He stirred; and beauty all at once
    Forth from His Being broke:
Spirit and strength, and living life,
    Created things, awoke.

Order, and multitude, and light,
    In beauteous showers out-stream'd;
And realms of newly-fashion'd space
    With radiant angels beam'd.

How wonderful is life in Heaven
    Amid the angelic choirs,
Where uncreated Love has crown'd
    His first created fires!

But see! new marvel s gather there!
    The wisdom of the Son
With Heaven's completest wonder ends
    The work so well begun.

The Throne is set: the blessed Three
    Crowning their work are seen—
The Mother of the First-Born Son,
    The first born creatures' Queen!

FAITH OF OUR FATHERS.

FAITH of our Fathers! living still,
    In spite of dungeon, fire, and sword:
Oh how our hearts beat high with joy
    Whene'er we hear that glorious word:
Faith of our Fathers! Holy Faith!
We will be true to thee till death!

Our Fathers, chain'd in prisons dark,
    Were still in heart and conscience free:
How sweet would be their children's fate,
    If they, like them, could die for thee!
Faith of our Fathers! Holy Faith!
We will be true to thee till death!

Faith of our Fathers! Mary's prayers
    Shall win our country all to thee;
And through the truth that comes from God
    Our land shall then indeed be free:
Faith of our Fathers! Holy Faith!
We will be true to thee till death!

Faith of our Fathers! we will love
    Both friend and foe in all our strife:
And preach thee too, as love knows how,
    By kindly words and virtuous life:
Faith of our Fathers! Holy Faith!
We will be true to thee till death!

THE RIGHT MUST WIN.

O IT is hard to work for God,
    To rise and take His part
Upon this battle-field of earth,
    And not sometimes lose heart!

He hides Himself so wondrously
    As though there were no God;
He is least seen when all the powers
    Of ill are most abroad;

Or He deserts us at the hour
    The fight is all but lost;
And seems to leave us to ourselves
    Just when we need Him most.

O there is less to try our faith,
    In our mysterious creed,
Than in the godless look of earth
    In these our hours of need.

Ill masters good; good seems to change
    To ill with greatest ease;
And, worst of all, the good with good
    Is at cross purposes.

The Church, the Sacraments, the Faith,
    Their up-hill journey take,
Lose here what there they gain, and, if
    We lean upon them, break.

It is not so, but so it looks;
    And we lose courage then;
And doubts will come if God hath kept
    His promises to men.

Ah! God is other than we think;
    His ways are far above,
Far beyond reason's height, and reach'd
    Only by childlike love.

The look, the fashion of God's ways
    Love's lifelong study are;
She can be bold, and guess, and act,
    When reason would not dare.

She has a prudence of her own;
    Her step is firm and free;
Yet there is cautious science too
    In her simplicity.

Workman of God! O lose not heart,
    But learn what God is like;
And in the darkest battle-field
    Thou shalt know where to strike.

O blest is he to whom is given
    The instinct that can tell
That God is on the field, when He
    Is most invisible!

And blest is he who can divine
    Where real right doth lie,
And dares to take the side that seems
    Wrong to man's blindfold eye!

O learn to scorn the praise of men!
    O learn to lose with God!
For Jesus won the world through shame,
    And beckons thee His road.

God's glory is a wondrous thing,
    Most strange in all its ways,
And, of all things on earth, least like
    What men agree to praise.

As He can endless glory weave
    From time's misjudging shame,
In His own world He is content
    To play a losing game.

Muse on His justice, downcast Soul!
    Muse and take better heart;
Back with thine angel to the field,
    Good luck shall crown thy part!

God's justice is a bed where we
    Our anxious hearts may lay,
And, weary with ourselves, may sleep
    Our discontent away.

For right is right, since God is God;
    And right the day must win;
To doubt would be disloyalty,
    To falter would be sin!

TRUE LOVE.

O SEE how Jesus trusts Himself
    Unto our childish love,
As though by His free ways with us
    Our earnestness to prove!

God gives Himself as Mary's Babe
    To sinners' trembling arms,
And veils His everlasting light
    In childhood's feeble charms.

His sacred Name a common word
    On earth He loves to hear;
There is no majesty in Him
    Which love may not come near.

His priests, they bear Him in their hands,
    Helpless as babe can be;
His love seems very foolishness
    For its simplicity.

The light of love is round His feet,
    His paths are never dim;
And He comes nigh to us when we
    Dare not come nigh to Him.

Let us be simple with Him then,
    Not backward, stiff, or cold,
As though our Bethlehem could be
    What Sina was of old.

His love of us may teach us how
    To love Him in return;
Love cannot help but grow more free
    The more its transports burn.

The solemn face, the downcast eye,
    The words constrain'd and cold,—
These are the homage, poor at best,
    Of those outside the fold.

They know not how our God can play
    The Babe's, the Brother's part;
They dream not of the ways He has
    Of getting at the heart.

Most winningly He lowers Himself,
    Yet they dare not come near;
They cannot know in their blind place
    The love that casts out fear.

In lowest depths of littleness
    God sinks to gain our love;
They put away the sign in fear,
    And our free ways reprove.

O that they knew what Jesus was,
    And what untold abyss
Lies in love's simple forwardness
    Of more than earthly bliss!

O that they knew what faith can work!
    What Sacraments can do!
What simple love is like, on fire
    In hearts absolved and true!

How can they tell how Jesus oft
    His secret thirst will slake
On those strange freedoms childlike hearts
    Are taught by God to take?

Poor souls! they know not how to love;
    They feel not Jesus near;
And they who know not how to love
    Still less know how to fear.

The humbling of the Incarnate Word
    They have not faith to face;
And how shall they who have not faith
    Attain love's better grace?

The awe that lies too deep for words,
    Too deep for solemn looks,—
It finds no way into the face,
    No spoken vent in books.

They would not speak in measured tones,
    If love had in them wrought,
Until their spirits had been hush'd
    In reverential thought.

They would have smiled in playful ways
    To ease their fervid heart,
And learn'd with other simple souls
    To play love's crafty part.

They would have run away from God
    For their own vileness' sake,
And fear'd lest some interior light
    From tell-tale eyes should break.

They know not how the outward smile
    The inward awe can prove;
They fathom not the creature's fear
    Of Uncreated Love.

The majesty of God ne'er broke
    On them like fire at night,
Flooding their stricken souls, while they
    Lay trembling in the light.

They love not; for they have not kiss'd
    The Saviour's outer hem:
They fear not for the Living God
    Is yet unknown to them!

PERFECTION.

O HOW the thought of God attracts
    And draws the heart from earth,
And sickens it of passing shows
    And dissipating mirth!

'Tis not enough to save our souls,
    To shun the eternal fires;
The thought of God will rouse the heart
    To more sublime desires.

God only is the creature's home,
    Though long and rough the road;
Yet nothing less can satisfy
    The love that longs for God.

O utter but the name of God
    Down in your heart of hearts,
And see how from the world at once
    All tempting light departs.

A trusting heart, a yearning eye,
    Can win their way above;
If mountains can be moved by faith,
    Is there less power in love?

How little of that road, my soul!
    How little hast thou gone!
Take heart, and let the thought of God
    Allure thee further on.

The freedom from all wilful sin,
    The Christian's daily task, —
O these are graces far below
    What longing love would ask!

Dole not thy duties out to God,
    But let thy hand be free
Look long at Jesus; His sweet Blood,
    How was it dealt to thee?

The perfect way is hard to flesh;
    It is not hard to love;
If thou wert sick for want of God
    How swiftly wouldst thou move!

Good is the cloister's silent shade,
    Cold watch and pining fast;
Better the mission's wearing strife,
    If there thy lot be cast.

Yet mine of these perfection needs: —
    Keep thy heart calm all day,
And catch the words the Spirit there
    From hour to hour may say.

O keep thy conscience sensitive;
    No inward token miss;
And go where grace entices thee; —
    Perfection lies in this.

Be docile to thine un seen Guide,
    Love Him as He loves thee;
Time and obedience are enough,
    And thou a Saint shalt be!

THE ETERNAL FATHER.

MY God! how wonderful Thou art,
    Thy Majesty, how bright!
How beautiful thy Mercy-Seat
    In depths of burning light!

How dread are thine eternal years,
    O everlasting Lord!
By prostrate spirits day and night
    Incessantly adored!

How beautiful, how beautiful
    The sight of Thee must be,
Thine endless wisdom, boundless power,
    And awful purity!

O how I fear Thee, Living God!
    With deepest, tenderest fears,
And worship Thee with trembling hope,
    And penitential tears.

Yet I may love Thee too, O Lord!
    Almighty as Thou art,
For Thou hast stoop'd to ask of me
    The love of my poor heart.

O then this worse than worthless heart
    In pity deign to take,
And make it love Thee, for thyself
    And for thy glory's sake.

No earthly father loves like Thee,
    No mother half so mild
Bears and forbears, as Thou hast done,
    With me thy sinful child.

Only to sit and think of God —
    O what a joy it is!
To think the thought, to breathe the name —
    Earth has no higher bliss;

Father of Jesus! love's reward!
    What rapture will it be,
Prostrate before thy throne to lie,
    And gaze and gaze on Thee!

JESUS RISEN.

ALL hail! dear Conqueror! all hail!
    O what a victory is thine!
How beautiful thy strength appears,
    Thy crimson wounds, how bright they shine!

Thou camest at the dawn of day;
    Armies of souls around Thee were,
Blest spirits, thronging to adore
    Thy Flesh, so marvelous, so fair.

The everlasting Godhead lay
    Shrouded within those limbs divine,
Nor left untenanted one hour
    That sacred Human Heart of thine.

They worshipp'd Thee, those ransom'd souls,
    With the fresh strength of love set free,
They worshipp'd joyously, and thought
    Of Mary while they look'd on Thee.

And Thou, too, Soul of Jesus! Thou
    Towards that sacred Flesh didst yearn,
And for the beatings of that Heart
    How ardently thy love did burn!

They worshipp'd, while the beauteous Soul
    Paused by the Body's wounded side: —
Bright flash'd the cave, — before them stood
    The Living Jesus Glorified.

Down, down, all lofty things on earth,
    And worship Him with joyous dread!
O Sin! thou art undone by love!
    O Death! thou art discomfited!

Ye Heavens, how sang they in your courts,
    How sang the angelic choirs that day,
When from His tomb the imprison'd God,
    Like the strong sunrise, broke away.

O, I am burning so with love,
    I fear lest I should make too free;
Let me lie silent and adore
    Thy glorified Humanity.

Ah! now Thou sendest me sweet tears;
    Flutter'd with love, my spirits fail,—
What shall I say? Thou know'st my heart;
    All hail! dear Conqueror! all hail!

THE APPARITION OF JESUS TO OUR BLESSED LADY.

O QUEEN of Sorrows! raise thine eyes!
    See! the first light of dawn is there;
The hour is come, and thou must end
    Thy Forty Hours of lonely prayer.

Day dawns; it brightens on the hill:
    New grace, new powers within her wake,
Lest the full tide of joy should crush
    The heart that sorrow could not break.

O never yet had Acts of Hope
    Been offer'd to the Throne on high,
Like those that died on Mary's lip,
    And beam'd from out her glistening eye.

Hush! there is silence in her heart,
    Deeper than when St. Gabriel spoke,
And upon midnight's tingling ear
    The blessed Ave sweetly broke.

Ah me! what wondrous change is this!
    What trembling floods of noiseless light!
Jesus before His Mother stands,
    Jesus, all beautiful and bright!

He comes! He comes! and will she run
    With freest love her Child to greet?
He came! and she, His creature, fell
    Prostrate at her Creator's feet.

He raised her up; He pressed her head
    Gently against His wounded side;
He gave her spirit strength to bear
    The sight of Jesus glorified.

From out His eyes, from out His wounds
    A power of awful beauty shone;
O how the speechless Mother gazed
    Upon the glory of her Son!

She could not doubt: 'twas truly He
    Who had been with her from the first, —
The very eyes, the mouth, the hair,
    The very Babe whom she had nursed, —

Her burden o'er the desert sands,
    The helpmate of her toils, — 'twas He,
He by whose deathbed she had stood
    Long hours beneath the bleeding Tree.

His crimson wounds, they shone like suns,
    His beaming hand was raised to bless;
The sweetness of His voice had hush'd
    The angels into silentness.

His sacred flesh, like spirit, glow'd,
    Glow'd with immortal beauty's might;
His smiles were like the virgin rays
    That sprang from new-created light.

When Wilt thou drink that beauty in?
    Mother! when wilt thou satisfy
With those adoring looks of love
    The thirst of thine ecstatic eye?

Not yet, not yet thy wondrous joy
    Is fill'd to its mysterious brim;
Thou hast another sight to see
    To which this vision is but dim!

Jesus into His Mother's heart
    A special gift of strength did pour,
That she might bear what none had borne
    Amid the sons of earth before.

O let not words be bold to tell
    What in the Mother's heart was done,
When for a moment Mary saw
    The unshrouded Godhead of her Son.

What bliss for us that Jesus gave
    To her such wondrous gifts and powers;
It is a joy the joys were hers,
    For Mary's joys are doubly ours!

CONVERSION.

O FAITH! thou workest miracles
    Upon the hearts of men,
Choosing thy home in those same hearts
    We know not how or when.

To one thy grave unearthly truths
    A heavenly vision seem;
While to another's eye they are
    A superstitious dream.

To one the deepest doctrines look
    So naturally true,
That when he learns the lesson first
    He hardly thinks it new.

To other hearts the selfsame truths
    No light or heat can bring;
They are but puzzling phrases strung
    Like beads upon a string.

O Gift of Gifts! O Grace of Faith!
    My God! how can it be
That Thou, who hast discerning love,
    Shouldst give that gift to me?

There was a place, there was a time,
    Whether by night or day,
Thy Spirit came and left that gift,
    And went upon His way.

How many hearts Thou mightst have had
    More innocent than mine!
How many souls more worthy far
    Of that sweet touch of thine!

Ah, Grace! into unlikeliest hearts
    It is thy boast to come,
The glory of thy light to find
    In darkest spots a home.

How will they die, how will they die,
    How bear the cross of grief,
Who have not got the light of faith,
    The courage of belief?

The crowd of cares, the weightiest cross
    Seem trifles less than light, —
Earth looks so little and so low,
    When faith shines full and bright.

O happy, happy that I am!
    If thou canst be, O Faith!
The treasure that thou art in life,
    What wilt thou be in death?

Thy choice, O God of Goodness! then
    I lovingly adore;
O give me grace to keep thy grace,
    And grace to merit more!

IN PRAISE OF THE HOLY CROSS.

COME, let us with glad music
    Extol the Holy Cross;
'Tis our especial glory,
    Exult we in the Cross
For by the Cross we triumph,
    Our foemen we destroy;
Its standard is our signal
    For victory and joy.

Now let our sweetest trilling
    Reach far into the skies:
The sweetest Wood shall merit
    The sweetest melodies:

Nor be our life in discord
    With what our voices sing,
These may not clash together,
    True symphony to bring.

All ye, the Cross's servants,
    Be in its praises rife;
Without the Cross ye perish,
    The fountain of your life;
"Hail, all the world's Salvation!"
    Your salutation be,
In loudest proclamation
    Of this all-healing Tree.

How blest, how bright this altar,
    Wherefrom salvation beams!
Pours down the Lamb upon it
    His Blood in ruddy streams:
The Lamb that hath no blemish,
    And from their inborn crime
Hath purified all ages
    Until the end of time!

Lo, here the sinners' ladder;
    For Christ, the King of Heaven
By it draws to Him all things
    Into his power given:
And with the Cross's banner
    The truth too is unfurl'd;
Its four points comprehending
    The confines of the world!

New sacraments are dawning,
    But still in types, that so
The Cross's bright religion

May blaze with temper'd glow:
Wood cast in it by Mose
　　Makes Mara's waters sweet;
Obeying wood, the flintstone
　　Pours water at his feet!

The master hath no safety
　　For his doom'd house, before
The Cross upon the lintel
　　Hath fortified the door:
The sword, on whosoever
　　Hath set his faith upon
This sign, hath lost its power, —
　　He saves alive his son!

'Twas when Sarephtha's widow,
　　Poor, weak, was gath'ring wood,
There came the hope of safety,
　　For nigh the prophet stood!
Of Wood the mystic virtue
　　Where is no faith to feel,
The cruise of oil avails not,
　　Nor handful yet of meal!

What sense beneath such figures
　　Lay hid in Holy Writ,
Is now reveal'd to Christians, —
　　The Cross's benefit:
Kings yield belief, and foemen
　　Bow to the Cross alone, —
Where Christ himself is captain,
　　A thousand flee from one!

The Cross makes strength the stronger,
　　It conquers without fail,

It heals the sick and feeble,
    It makes the demons quail,
It gives to captives freedom,
    With new life it endues;
The dignity of all things
    The Cross again renews!

O Cross, thou Tree triumphal,
    Earth's sure Salvation, hail!
In stem, and leaf, and flower
    No tree's of thy avail!
The health art thou of Christians,
    Their medicine, if ill;
When human help is helpless,
    Be our protection still!

Hear all thy Cross's praises,
    Thou Hallower of the Cross,
Nor let thy Cross's servants
    Hereafter suffer loss;
But in the true Light's mansions,
    Departed hence, appear,
Where God himself their light is,
    And dried is ev'ry tear!

If thou assign us torture,
    Let torture not be felt;
But when Wrath's day is instant,
    Be mercy to us dealt!
To thee, against th' oppressor,
    Confirm our last appeal,
And quickly let us enter
    Our everlasting weal!

LIFE, PASSION, AND MERITS OF CHRIST.

PART I.

FATHER of highest majesty,
    Remember all thy love,
That gave this wretched world thy Son
    From thy bright throne above;
Down from the seat of Godhead sent
To this poor place of banishment!

Remember Jesus Christ, to Thee
    Coequal though begot,
Took on Himself a servant's form.
    When born in lowly cot,
And Circumcision's law of sin
Obey'd, our ruin'd souls to win!

Remember how, when He was born,
    And on mean straw was laid,
From distant East the royal three
    Him mystic honor paid;
And aged Simeon's prophecy, —
His Mother's sword when he should die!

Remember Herod, who his God
    Like criminal pursued,
Sad mothers of their babes bereft
    In day that Rama rued;
The anguish that his parents wrought
The hours their truant Son they sought.

Remember, Father meek, the thirst,
    The hunger, cold, and heat,
That weigh'd upon his mortal Frame,

And wore his weary Feet:
His faintness through long toiling hours,
Each day exposed to winds and show'rs!

Remember all the pains that He
    Endured in labor's round,
To teach thy ways to little ones,
    Who in them wisdom found:
The sick relieved, till evening's close,
His nights of prayer denied repose!

PART II.

Remember how their Master knelt
    At his disciples' feet,
And washing them, a lesson taught
    For love's sweet service meet:
How, all devoted to their good,
He gave Himself to be their food!

Remember all his sorrow, when
    He in the garden pray'd,
The grief, the anguish, and the dread,
    Upon his spirit laid;
Was ever agony so sore,
That sweated Blood from ev'ry pore!

Remember by what treach'rous craft,
    And soldiers' arm'd array,
With meekest look that gentle Lamb
    Was led in cords away;
Like doer vile of envious wrong,
Dragg'd pris'ner by the guards along!

Remember, Jesus blindfold stood,
    Mid fierce and cruel bands,

Who, mocking, bade Him prophesy,
    And struck with impious hands;
How buffeted He lay forlorn,
    Stretch'd on the pavement, bruised and torn!

Remember what a crown they press'd
    Upon his sacred Head, —
That Head, which ev'ry gift enfolds,
    With thorny cincture bled;
How spit on, stripp'd, with scourges flay'd,
In purple robe He stood array'd!

Remember how He walk'd despised,
    In modest robe of white,
By naughty men accused for naught,
    His bounty to requite;
How they deliver'd the unjust
Barabbas, and condemn'd the Just!

PART III.

Remember what a weight the Cross
    Upon His shoulder lay,
So vast the crime of all the world,
    The load He bore away:
How impious men the Cross upon
Nail'd ruthlessly the guiltless One!

Remember, He, like helpless worm,
    Not man, was raised on high,
Mark for each finger, left as one
    No pity claim'd, to die:
Like one accurst, with anguish wrung,
Unconquer'd conqu'ror, thus He hung!

Remember how thy Heaven-sent Son
    Burn'd with devouring zeal,
And all our shame endured, that He
    Our shameful guilt might heal:
Of Mother's love, how great the grief,
To see her Son past all relief!

Remember with what wondrous love
    The robber He received,
Blest partner of his Passion made,
    Its power who believed!
His cup of vinegar and gall, —
The dregs of woe, He drank them all!

Remember all his fluttering dread,
    Of comfort when bereft,
"Why thus, my God," the Saviour cried,
    "Forsaken am I left?"
How shook the earth, day turn'd to night,
When from the world death took its Light!

Remember what a gory stream
    Burst from her dear Son's Heart,
With Water flowing and with Blood,
    Pierced by the soldier's dart:
How pierced the Mother standing by
The sword of her Son's agony!

Remember how, with bitter cry,
    Bereft ones mourn'd their loss;
While his cold Corpse, divine in death,
    They lower'd from the Cross;
And what a grief it was t' inter
That Body in the sepulchre!

Remember, we implore Thee, why
    'Twas thy own sacred Will,

Nor less thy Son's, for Him to feel
    Such insult, pain, and ill:
From glory, majesty, and power,
    Equal to thine, Himself to lower!

What force hath drawn that spotless Lamb,
    What mighty strength of love,
To come the guilty's doom to bear
    From those bright realms above?
'Tis boundless charity's sure sign,
The token true of love divine!

Then let thy love that thus hath been
    So fruitful, Lord, in pains,
Be fruitful to remove our sins,
    And wash out all their stains:
Love! strike deep root in all our hearts,
Engender'd thus of Jesus' smarts. Amen.

PRAYER ON GOING TO SLEEP.

PRAYER BEFORE A PICTURE OF OUR BLESSED LADY.

MOTHER! to thee myself I yield,
    Console me in the hour of pain;
Be thou my life's support and shield,
    And by me, at my death, remain!

PRAYER ON RISING IN THE MORNING.

Dear Jesu! as I wake be nigh;
    Inspire me, as I ought, to pray:
Keep me from Sin, O Lord most high,
    Through this and every other day.

To God the Father glory be,
  And to his sole-begotten Son;
The same, O Holy Ghost! to Thee,
  While everlasting ages run.

PRAYER ON GOING TO SLEEP.

ANGEL Guardian! guard me sleeping,
  Still unto God's service wake me
Loving watches o'er me keeping,
  In thy arms, dear Jesus, take me.

Honor, majesty, and power,
  To the blessed Three be given;
Father, Son, and Holy Ghost,
  Glory in the highest Heaven.

PRAYER TO A GUARDIAN ANGEL.

ANGEL! whom God
    Has appointed for me,
Of his mercy supreme,
    My Guardian to be:
My way through this world
    Light thou and protect;
Through this world to Heaven
    Forever direct.   *Amen.*

ANGELE Dei
Qui custos es mei
Me tibi commissum,
Pietate superna
Illumina, custodi
Rege et guberna.
            Amen.

DOXOLOGY.

To God the Father glory be,
    And to his sole-begotten Son
The same, O Holy Ghost, to Thee,
    While everlasting ages run.

    DEO Patri sit gloria,
    Ejus que soli Filio,
    Cum Spiritu Paraclito,
    Nunc et per omne saeculum.

www.ingramcontent.com/pod-product-compliance
Lightning Source LLC
Chambersburg PA
CBHW020422010526
44118CB00010B/369